K-12 Web Pages: Planning & Publishing Excellent School Web Sites

by Debra Kay Logan and Cynthia Beuselinck

PROFESSIONAL GROWTH SERIES®

A Publication of THE BOOK REPORT & LIBRARY TALK

Linworth Publishing, Inc.
Worthington, Ohio

" Minnetonka Community Education & Services - Community Resource Program" reprinted with the permission of Jose Nunez, Instructional Technology Coordinator, Minnetonka Public Schools.

" Mt. Laurel Hartford School's Library Without Walls" reprinted with the permission of Shane Russell, Educational Media Specialist, Mount Laurel Hartford School.

"Victoria School of Performing and Visual Arts" reprinted with the permission of Robert Wallace, Victoria School.

"Payson High School – Mr. Pauley's Site" reprinted with the permission of Joe Pauley, Payson High School.

"American Biographies" reprinted with the permission of Eric Lundman, Gotha Middle School.

"Montgomery County Public Schools Web Site Database" reprinted with the permission of David Kreisberg, Montgomery County Public Schools.

"St. Michael's School" reprinted with the permission of Bob Jackman and Barb Leyte, Goose Bay, St. Michael's School.

"Northmount School - Once upon a science story" reprinted with the permission of Duane Schade, Northmount School.

"Rusk Independent School Division - Online Lesson Plans and Homework " reprinted with the permission of Kara Bowling, Rusk Independent School Division.

"Create a State Project" reprinted with the permission of Karen Biddinger, F.V. Evans Elementary School.

"Alvirne High School - AP Calculus Problem of the Week" reprinted with the permission of Sandra Ray, Alvirne High School.

"Mount Pleasant - Ancient Images" reprinted with the permission of Beth Smithson, Mount Pleasant Elementary School.

"Buckman School - Dr. King Timeline" reprinted with the permission of Tim Lauer, Instructional Technology, Portland Public Schools.

"Nueva Parents Association" reprinted with the permission of Dana Eckert, Nueva School Parents Association.

"Arbor Heights Elementary School Archives" reprinted with the permission of Mark Ahlness, Arbor Heights Elementary School.

"Deb Logan's Web Page Tutorial" reprinted with the permission of Deb Logan.

"Montgomery County Public Schools - WebSmarts" reprinted with the permission of Aimee Timmins and Nancy Carey, Montgomery County Public Schools.

"Crofton House School - Who's Who Page" reprinted with the permission of Marcelle Adam/ Pinnacles & Prisms, Crofton School.

"A WebQuest About Evaluating Web Sites " reprinted with the permission of Joyce Valenza, Springfield Township High School.

"Mill Hill School - Mrs. Healey's Class" reprinted with the permission of Paula Healey, Mill Hill School.

"Lawrence High School Library" reprinted with the permission of Martha Oldman, Librarian, Lawrence High School.

Cataloging-in-Publication Data

Logan, Debra Kay, 1958-
    K-12 web pages : planning & publishing excellent school web sites / by Debra Kay
Logan and Cynthia Beuselinck.
        p.cm. — (Professional growth series)
      ISBN 1-58683-036-8 (perfect bound)
Internet in education—Study and teaching. 2. Web sites—Design—Study and
    teaching. 3. World Wide Web—Study and teaching. I. Beuselinck, Cynthia, 1962- II.
    Title. III. Series.

LB1044.87 .L64 2001
371.33'44678—dc21   2001038837

Published by Linworth Publishing, Inc.
480 East Wilson Bridge Road, Suite L
Worthington, Ohio 43085

ISBN 1-58683-036-8
5 4 3 2 1

Table of Contents

ABOUT THE AUTHORS iv
ACKNOWLEDGMENTS v
INTRODUCTION vii
    The Beginnings of This Book vii
    Why This Book? A Need for Direction vii
    Information That Provides Direction. viii
    How This Book Is Organized. viii
    Using This Book x

CHAPTER 1   **Why Create School & Educational Web Sites?** 1
    Why Did the Chicken... 1
    Community Connections. 1
    Partnerships with Parents 3
    Linking to Learners and Learning 4
    Engaging Educators 5
    Just the Beginning... 6

CHAPTER 2   **How to Get from Idea to Web Site: Beginning Steps** 7
    Web Planning Team 8
    Why, Who, and What?. 8
       Why. 9
       Who. 9
       What 10
    Put It in Writing... 11
    Exploring Possible Educational Web Pages and Then Getting Down to Business:
       Foundations for Informed Decision-Making. 11
    Checking Out Policy, Copyright, Support, and Technical Considerations 12

CHAPTER 3   **Possible Pages . . . What Goes on an Educational Web Site?** 13
    Content! Content! Content! 13
    Basics & Types. 14
       Informative Pages 14
       Curricular Pages 18
       Showcase Pages 20
       Revenue Generation Pages: A New Dimension of Educational Web Sites: 22
    Ideas in Action: Pulling It All Together. 23

CHAPTER 4   **Blueprints for a Firm Foundation: Publishing Guidelines and Policies** 31
    Design and Technical Guidelines 33
       Consistency 33
       Minimizing Download Times 34
       Accessibility Requirements 34
       Restricting File Types 35
    Content Guidelines 35
    Commercial Content. 38
    Safety and Liability Guidelines 39
       Personal Information 40
       Publishing the Work of Students 42
       Publishing Work Created by Volunteers or Staff Members 43
    Responsibility Guidelines 45
    Keeping the Guidelines and Policies Current 45
    Adding Disclaimers. 47
    The Rules of the Road . . . Protecting or Restricting? 48

CHAPTER 5   **Copyright Issues and the Web** 49
    What? It Isn't All "Free"! 49
    What Does This Mean for Educational Web Sites? 51
    Gray Areas. 54
       Links 54
       HTML 54

Table of Contents continued

Taking Steps to Protect School Districts and Web Sites 55
    A Safe Harbor for the District: Online Service Providers' Liability 55
    Protecting Web Sites: 56
Beyond Fines and Penalties 57

CHAPTER 6   **Gathering Resources . . . Just Who Is Needed?** 61
Who's in Charge Here? 61
Who Is Responsible for the Web Server(s)? 62
    District Servers 63
    School-Based Servers. 63
    Public Servers 63
Whom Do Schools Contact for Help? 65
    District Support Specialists 65
    Local Support Specialists 65
Responsibility for Training 66
Responsibility for Security 68
Responsibility for Policy & Guidelines 69
Responsibility for Content 69
Responsibility for Uploading 70
Responsibility for Growth and Future Planning 71
Creating Web Teams 71

CHAPTER 7   **Technical Considerations** 75
Finding a Home of Your Own: Where Will the Site Be Hosted? 76
Selecting Software Tools 77
    Authoring Tools 78
    Graphics and Compression Tools 78
    Site Management, Maintenance, and Statistical Tools 78
Understanding Space Allocations 79
Organizing and Naming Files and Folders 80
Serving Up Pages Fast! 81
Loading Restrictions 82
Linking, Moving, and Removing Pages 83
Putting the House in Order 84

CHAPTER 8   **Making It Real: From Goals to Content** 85
Making a Plan 85
Collecting and Creating Content 86

CHAPTER 9   **What Makes a Well-Designed Educational Web Site?** 87
Basic Beginnings . . . Beginning at the End 87
Step One: Assuring Access 90
    Accessibility 90
    Site Structure 92
    Navigation 95
    Page Layout 96
Step Two: Functional Formats 99
    Images 99
    Color 100
    Text 102
Step Three: Creating Content 103
    Links 103
    Writing 104
    Authority 104
    Multimedia 105
When to Break the Rules 105
Breaking the Rules! 106
Is It Done Yet? 106

CHAPTER 10   **The Never-ending Journey** 107
Promotion 107
    Working with the Press 108
    Making Search Engine Hit Lists 109
Education 110

Evaluation 110
Maintenance 110
Revision 111

APPENDIX 1:   **Web Planning and Check Sheets** 113

District Web Planning Team Information Sheet 114
School Web Planning Team Information Sheet 115
Web Site Vision Statement Worksheet 116
Technical Support Resource List 118
Publishing Guidelines and Policies Check Sheet 120
Web Team Decision-Planning Sheet: Questions to Consider When Making
      Recommendations and Setting Goals 124
Web Site Goals Worksheet 127
Web Site Objectives Worksheet 128
Informative Educational Web Pages Planning Sheet 129
Curricular Pages Planning Sheet 132
Showcase Pages Planning Sheet 133
Revenue Generation Pages Planning Sheet 134
Evaluating Web Sites for Linking 135
Copyright Check Sheet 137
Technical Considerations & Constraints Check Sheet 139
Design Check Sheet 140
File Name Worksheet 145
Image Source Note Sheet 146
Prepublication Check Sheet 147
Promotion Check Sheet 148
Evaluation Planning Sheet 150
Web Site Evaluation Form 151
Maintenance Check Sheet 152

APPENDIX 2:   **Where to Go for Additional Help and Resources** 153

General Web Builder Resource Sites 154
Software Archives 154
Software and Hardware Reviews 155
Organizations and Help for Web Builders 155
Scripts 156
Graphics & Color 156
Validation Tools 157
Log Analysis Programs and Services 157
Add-Ons 158
      General Collections 158
      Communications 158
Other Tools 159
School Site Awards–For Inspiration and Encouragement 159

GLOSSARY 161
WORKS CITED AND SELECTED RECOMMENDED RESOURCES LIST 168
INDEX 175

About the Authors

DEB LOGAN is the Librarian/Media Specialist for Mount Gilead High School in Mount Gilead, Ohio. Prior to holding this position, Logan spent 13 years with the Marion (Ohio) City Schools, most recently at Taft Middle School. She majored in library educational media at Bowling Green State University (Bowling Green, Ohio) and has an M.L.S. from the University of Arizona at Tucson. She began her professional career as a children's librarian. Her career has also included adult reference work and experience in an elementary school library media center. She has been a KidsConnect volunteer since 1997 and is a member of the InfOhio Web Accessibility Committee.

Logan is the author of *Information Skills Toolkit: Collaborative Integrated Instruction for the Middle Grades* (Linworth, 2000) and the *Got Books Turnkey Kit* (American Dairy Association & Dairy Council Mid East, 2000). She has contributed to *The Book Report, Library Talk, Knowledge Quest, Ohio Media Spectrum, Today's School Media Specialist, Skills for Life: K–6 Second Edition,* and *Skills for Life: 7–12 Second Edition.* The author also presents at conferences and is involved in a variety of professional organizations. Her Taft Library Media Center Web site < http://www.infotaft.marioncity.k12.oh.us/index.html> was named the June 1999 School Library Journal Online Web Site of the Month. Logan is also the webmaster of the Taft Middle School Web Site <http://www.bakerms.marioncity.k12.oh.us/taft/index.html> and deblogan.com <http://www.deblogan.com>. A Mount Gilead High School Library site is being planned at this time. Logan can be reached at *deb@deblogan.com.*

CYNTHIA BEUSELINCK is a graduate of the Library and Information Technology program at the Southern Alberta Institute of Technology (SAIT) in Calgary, Alberta and is pursuing a B.P.A. in communications through Athabasca University via distance education. From 1996 to 2000, she was the Internet Support Specialist for the Calgary Board of Education, the largest school district in western Canada. She provided 30 to 50 hours per month of Internet training for more than 400 Web Administrators, along with professional development days for other staff members in the district.

Beuselinck worked in libraries almost a decade before she moved into a related career in information technology. She now owns her own computer and Internet training company that specializes in educational environments. Through various workshops, presentations, and tutoring, she has helped hundreds of school webmasters tackle and manage issues surrounding the development of school sites and student projects for the Web.

Beuselinck is a past president of the Alberta Association of Library Technicians (AALT), was on the Future of School Libraries Task Force for the Calgary Board of Education, and continues to be involved with library organizations through her professional memberships. She has been a regular contributor to the *AALT Journal* since 1995 and is currently the moderator for the Alberta School Web Authors and Administrators forum in Alberta, Canada. A dynamic presenter during her workshops and conference sessions, Cynthia encourages and inspires her students with her enthusiasm. She can be reached at *cynthia@inet-toolbox.com.*

Acknowledgments

Many individuals have generously given their time and expertise during the writing of this book. The authors wish to begin by thanking Diane Kovacs for her vision in bringing us together to work on this book. We appreciate the excellent advice, support, and encouragement provided by our editor, Betty Morris. Wendy Medvetz's expertise is also appreciated. Thank you to Linworth's Marlene Woo-Lun, Amy Robison, Amy Murch, "The Donnas," and the reviewers.

Cynthia Beuselinck would like to thank Jack Dale and George Veenhuysen for sharing their expertise on safety issues, and Joe Czentye for extensive technical guidance. The Web Administrators at the Calgary Board of Education deserve a special thank you; working with that dedicated group of school Web site builders made the information in this book live research instead of just theory. Cynthia would also like to thank the many friends, colleagues, and family members who were a constant source of encouragement and support, and Deb Logan for her patience and direction throughout this project.

Deb Logan extends personal thanks to experts Carol Simpson, John Shank, Barb Drake, Michael G. Paiciello, InfOhio's Web Accessibility Committee, Diane Kovacs, and Bill Born for special information and advice. She offers special thanks to Jeff Logan and Sandy Winland, who gave extra support during the writing of this book.

> Deb Logan's work on this book is dedicated with love to
> Jeffrey A. Logan (1947–2001),
> whose love, patience, humor, sense of fun, pride, kindness,
> and generosity made this book possible.

Introduction

*Organizing is what you do before you do something,
so that when you do it, it is not all mixed up.*

—A. A. Milne

▶ THE BEGINNINGS OF THIS BOOK

This book is the culmination of many years of work by the authors on school Web sites. Like most school Web site builders, both authors began looking for answers to questions about content, design, safety, ethics, and responsibility. The task of finding the answers to critical questions about what should and should not be on a school Web page soon evolved into a quest. Logan and Beuselinck met many others online who were searching for the same answers. The information is out there, but is scattered throughout books, journal articles, and Web sites. Locating and organizing the information is a major and time-consuming task. Many times along the way, the authors thought, "This is so important and so many people are looking for it—why isn't there a book with all this information in one place?" The idea to create such a resource grew out of this question.

▶ WHY THIS BOOK? A NEED FOR DIRECTION

The great news about the creation of Web sites is that it is not "rocket science." Educators can quickly and easily create and post Web sites to the Internet to reach out to students, colleagues, parents, and their communities. The not-so-great news is that the rush to publish on the Internet has resulted in the publication of resources of varying quality, reliability, usability, appropriateness, safety, and even legality. The ease of Web publishing sometimes means a lack of planning and the omission of the types of prepublication scrutiny and revision that are routinely part of traditional publishing processes. Though they are launched into a global environment, school Web sites often are developed with a local mindset. Global publishing differs significantly from the local newsletters and handbooks typically published by educators. It involves different laws and brings up different issues. Some educators may not be certain of even what questions they should be asking in order to plan and publish excellent school Web sites.

This resource book is intended for teachers, district technology departments, school librarians/media specialists, and school administrators at all levels of Web publishing sophistication. The information will help all educators—the ones who know the questions to ask as well as those who are unsure. The book is designed to help answer those questions by providing information and explanations on which to base decisions. It supports informed planning and decision making.

▶ INFORMATION THAT PROVIDES DIRECTION

K–12 Web Pages: Planning & Publishing Excellent School Web Sites gathers, examines, and organizes the results of the authors' efforts to uncover the best educational practices in Web publishing. This book does not focus on how to build Web pages step-by-step or how to use software packages. Instead, it helps educators define and answer their questions about the preparation needed to build high quality, low risk, and meaningful educational Web sites as it guides them through the process of planning an educational Web site. The vital roles, responsibilities, and possible liabilities of administration as they relate to Web site technical issues, policies, and decision-making are explored. The book presents safe and responsible Web publishing practices that will provide creative learning opportunities without jeopardizing students, teachers, schools, or others in the process.

The book also examines Web planning from different perspectives. These range from the relatively simple process of one individual creating Web resources for a classroom to the more complex planning processes needed for many people to develop a school or district Web site. The authors have firsthand knowledge of Web site development at individual, school, and district levels. Beuselinck has the perspective of supporting and developing Web sites in a well-supported and technically sophisticated environment while Logan has approached publishing Web sites in a relatively small school district with minimal support. Both have spent years looking at school Web sites and locating information on how to make them better. The authors hope to pass on what they have learned to teachers, district technology departments, and school administrators through this book. This book's goal is to provide those who work with students a set of Web publishing "best practices" for teaching and learning with one of the greatest technological tools in schools today.

▶ HOW THIS BOOK IS ORGANIZED

K–12 Educator's Web Page Planning & Publishing Kit begins with the introductory materials, which are followed by ten chapters, two appendixes, a glossary, a resource list, and an index.

CHAPTER 1: *Why Create School & Educational Web Sites?*
When planning to publish on the Internet, educators need to think about their reasons for publishing. In the past, schools did just fine without a Web site. Is the amount of planning, the work involved in building and maintaining the site, and the cost of all that technology really necessary? What can be accomplished via this type of resource? The first chapter explores the reasons educators publish on the Internet. This exploration is crucial to planning a school Web site.

CHAPTER 2: *How to Get from Idea to Web Site: Beginning Steps*

Where should Web creators start? The information in Chapter 2 outlines first steps toward the development of an educational Web site. Follow the suggestions in this chapter when forming a Web planning team and creating a vision statement.

CHAPTER 3: *Possible Pages . . . What Goes on an Educational Web Site?*

What kinds of information can be found on educational Web pages? What types of educational Web sites and pages are possible? Explore ways to accomplish the goals of a Web site by looking in this chapter. This chapter divides educational Web pages into four categories: Informational, Curricular, Showcase, and Revenue Generation.

CHAPTER 4: *Blueprints for a Firm Foundation: Publishing Guidelines and Policies*

After looking at reasons for publishing on the Internet, educators need to think about safety and ethical, legal, and administrative issues. These questions need to be asked early in the planning process. One of the first questions should be "What can be published on the Internet without placing students and staff at risk?" This critical administrative chapter covers red-hot policy issues such as liability, student safety, and permission forms.

CHAPTER 5: *Copyright Issues and the Web*

Another high-priority question is "What can be published legally on the Internet?" Educators are asking, "What are the copyright laws that pertain to Internet publishing?" Look here for information about how copyright impacts the use of materials on and from the Web. Find out how to protect materials posted to the Web from copyright violations.

CHAPTER 6: *Gathering Resources . . . Just Who Is Needed?*

Administrators need to look at a variety of pragmatic Web publishing questions. "Who will be responsible for creating and maintaining Web pages?" and "Who should deal with content challenges?" are just two of the questions. This chapter looks at administrative issues, such as who needs to be involved in and responsible for the Web servers, creating Web teams, technical support, future planning, security, and growth.

CHAPTER 7: *Technical Considerations*

Administrative questions can be complex; for example, "Where will the Web sites be housed?" or "What kind of additional software tools are needed?" This chapter examines technical considerations, such as management of files and folders, Web site housing, space allocations, and loading restrictions as well as managing pages, software, and links.

CHAPTER 8: *Making It Real: From Goals to Content*

Once educators have gathered information, they are ready to make decisions and to set goals and objectives. It is time to make a plan. This short chapter guides Web planners through the decision-making and planning process. It also looks at beginning to gather content for the Web site.

CHAPTER 9: *What Makes a Well-Designed Educational Web Site?*

Prior to publishing on the Web, educators need to ask questions related to Web design: "How can a Web site be made accessible?" "How will users move about the site?" "What will be 'the look' of the site and why?" "How will information be arranged on the site and how will it be written?" Chapter 9 helps educators design Web pages that are meaningful, appealing, distinctive, usable, and readable. Whole books have been dedicated to the topic of Web design. This chapter identifies and highlights critical planning decisions relating to the kinds of issues that are essential elements of well-designed Web sites.

CHAPTER 10: *The Never Ending Journey*

The page is on the Web! Is it done? What should happen next? Chapter 10 looks at promotion, education, evaluation, and maintenance. There is no such thing as "done" in Web work.

APPENDIX 1: *Web Planning and Check Sheets*

This appendix pulls together a plethora of resource tools, such as planning and check sheets. These sheets complement and supplement information found in all ten of the book's chapters. Copy the worksheets to use as planning tools and to check process and progress.

APPENDIX 2: *Where to Go for Additional Help and Resources*

This array of helpful lists of resources will assist in the planning and creation of educational Web sites.

GLOSSARY, WORKS CITED, AND SELECTED REECOMMENDED RESOURCES LIST

The glossary defines technical terms used in this book. The bibliography provides citations for works quoted and for works that contributed to the content of this book. An index completes the work.

▷ USING THIS BOOK

Like the Web itself, the process of creating a Web page is interconnected. Many of the topics covered in this book overlap and have connections throughout the book. When appropriate, connections are referenced. *Resource Boxes*, scattered throughout this book, are mini-collections of helpful materials that are related to specific topics. Check out the *Quick Tip* boxes for proven ideas that will be helpful during the process of Web planning and creation. *Fast Fact* boxes contain additional or explanatory information. Read the *Ideas in Action* sections to find out how other educational institutions have managed their Web site planning processes.

Chapter 1

Why Create School & Educational Web Sites?

'Tis true: there's magic in the web of it...

—William Shakespeare
Othello *Act 3, Scene 4*

▶ WHY DID THE CHICKEN . . .

Why create school and educational Web sites? There are about as many answers to that question as there are to "Why did the chicken cross the road?" The answers to both questions can be practical, profound, philosophical, intentionally hilarious, and "groaners." Sometimes the answer to both questions has been "Because it's there" or "Because it (we) can." If an educational site is created for these reasons, the results may make people groan. This chapter looks at meaningful reasons for educators to publish on the Internet and how to begin to create a vision for educational Web publishing.

When beginning to think about creating an educational Web site, the place to start is the intended audience. With this in mind, this chapter is organized by possible audiences under the headings *Community Connections, Partnerships with Parents, Linking to Learners and Learning,* and *Engaging Educators.*

▶ COMMUNITY CONNECTIONS

Wait a minute! Aren't educational Web sites for children? Even when school Web pages appear to be geared toward teachers, parents, alumni, the community, or a more global audience, the ultimate answer to "Why create educational Web sites?" is usually child-centered. However, this does not mean that the content should be intended only for children.

Figure 1.1 Minnetonka Community Education & Services—Community Resource Program

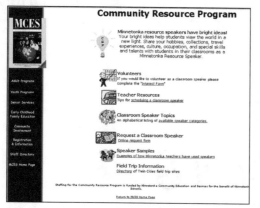

<http://www.minnetonka.k12.mn.us/mces/crp/index.htm>

This page highlights community connections by encouraging community members to share their experiences and participate as classroom speakers. *Jose Nunez, Instructional Technology Coordinator, Minnetonka Public Schools, Minnetonka, Minnesota*

Schools and school systems do not operate in isolation—it does take a village to raise a child. Community support is crucial in education. Educators are working to form partnerships with individuals, community businesses, other educational groups, and community organizations. These partnerships can be used to share expertise, resources, and services. Some partnerships may involve contact with students in the form of mentoring and tutoring programs. Even these personal contacts can be facilitated through the use of Web resources. The Web has great potential to support the efforts of educators to reach out to their communities in order to better serve their students.

Funding and other forms of support come from a variety of levels and avenues. The time to start campaigning for financial or other support is before the need arises. Communication is one of the strongest forms of prevention. Educators who share what is good about their schools and who become integral parts of the community are less likely to have to create a positive image on short notice. This proactive type of public relations has other advantages. Educators who are involved in a story are often in a better position to be more accurate than outside sources. People who have been interviewed by outside reporters are usually aware that even good reporters make errors or tell stories in awkward ways. Educators can ensure that school Web sites focus on the positive.

FAST FACT

More and more school districts are using school Web sites as a source of revenue.

Including commercial banners and links is just one way to generate revenue with an educational Web site. Some districts have policies that do not permit the inclusion of commercial content. Check district's Web publishing guidelines before placing fund-raising content on an educational Web page.

FAST FACT

Educational Web sites are cost-effective marketing tools.

They are not "here and gone" like newspaper, radio, and television stories. There are no per-page printing and paper costs. They are easily updated at a relatively low cost.

A school Web site can be viewed as a community resource that can be tapped at any time for support and guidance. It can demonstrate to a community that people in a school have initiative, are caring, are diverse, and are mindful of the importance of the community as a whole. Creating a school or a district Web site that informs, supports, and involves community stakeholders is being proactive on behalf of students. School Web sites can provide virtual libraries that link to community and regional resources on topics such as parenting, helping children with homework, health issues, and career counseling. School districts can put together resources such as an online speakers' bureau. Use school Web sites to showcase and share community assets and news. If strong guidelines are in place, schools may consider hosting sites for local organizations, such as "Friends of the Library," scout troops, and parent organizations. This type of service on school Web sites can add a new dimension to the way that community members and parents view the school. By involving the community in educational Web sites, schools are ultimately serving their students.

▶ PARTNERSHIPS WITH PARENTS

Educators need to communicate with parents to be effective with children. A school Web site can also help by providing opportunities for parents to participate in their children's education without traveling to school or playing telephone tag. Some schools have password-protected areas that allow parents to check the progress of their children online at any time instead of waiting for report cards or relying on the children for the information. Doug Johnson, in "Teacher Web Pages That Build Parent Partnerships" (*MultiMedia Schools*, September 2000), provides a familiar scenario:

> Just think. Junior comes home, plopping down on the sofa with remote in hand. "How's the homework situation?" you ask. "Under control. Got it all done in study

hall," replies Junior. You double-check by logging on to the class Web page, enter your personal username and password, and find that Junior has been missing daily assignments and did not do well on the last test. The assessment checklist for a big project that is due soon is there, too. Ah, something to talk about at suppertime.

Figure 1.2 Mt. Laurel Hartford School's Library Without Walls

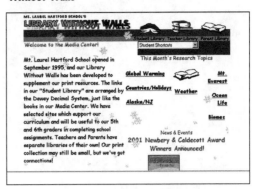

`<http://209.27.186.150/mc/index.html>`
Not only has this school media center created excellent curricular support areas for teachers and students, but it also provides support resources for its parent community.
Shane Russell, Educational Media Specialist, Mount Laurel Hartford School, Mt. Laurel, New Jersey

While a Web page is not meant to replace the face-to-face interaction of parent-teacher meetings, it can go a long way toward fine-tuning those meetings and addressing student needs more quickly. The school Web site can add a valuable opportunity for parents to be involved with their child's day-to-day schoolwork. A school Web site can demonstrate to parents that the school is looking for flexible ways to help them participate in and support the learning process.

When considering reasons for creating school Web pages, do not forget the dilemma of the "backpack black hole." Educators and parents are aware of the masses of papers, forms, notes, messages, and other vital communications that traditionally have been placed in children's hands to be taken home. These often disappear into backpacks never to be seen again. The backpack phenomenon could be solved in part by giving parents the option of downloading these types of communications from the Web or via other forms of online communication systems.

Parents should be able to turn to the school Web site for resources and to become more involved with the school as a parent. Single-parent and even two-parent households are feeling an enormous time crunch that impacts how much time parents spend with their kids. Collections of parenting resources can be extremely helpful to parents who are turning to the Web for information.

Parents have increasing numbers of options for educating their children. They can choose public, private, vocational, charter, home, or virtual (online) schools. Schools are often in a position of having to woo parents into considering them a viable and worthwhile choice for their educational dollars. Families who are faced with moves to new communities are shopping for schools. Often, parents can begin their research process through accessing the school Web site. Parents want high quality schools that are responsible, caring, and informed. Parents want to know that the school will welcome them as a part of their child's educational process. They want to see schools that are preparing their children for the future. Parents often equate the use of technology with quality. School Web sites can provide all this information all the time. School Web sites are not just an incidental information resource, but are a continuous marketing vehicle that should provide the best reflection of what the school has to offer students.

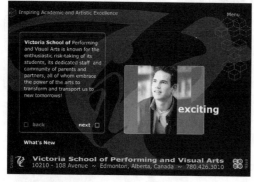

Figure 1.3 Victoria School of Performing and Visual Arts

<http://victoria.epsb.net/>
Impressive design and full multimedia are hallmarks of this K–12 school Web site. An impressive marketing tool and showcase for student work, this site leaves no doubt that Victoria is an innovative arts school. *Vic New Media Web team, led by teacher Robert Wallace, Edmonton, Alberta, Canada*

➤ LINKING TO LEARNERS AND LEARNING

Students are not intimidated by technology; they are mesmerized by it. Educational Web sites can heighten student interest in learning. A school Web site with discussion areas, interactive features, simulations, relevant content, or meaningful links to the good resources on the Web motivates students to want to explore and learn more. The multimedia nature of the Internet allows educators to create or link to a variety of resources aimed at students' individual learning styles and needs. Educators who are seeking to provide students with authentic learning situations can use the Web to bring the real world into schools and children's homes every day. An educational Web site can facilitate and personalize these processes through the use of student- or teacher-created online resources, such as WebQuests, virtual experiences, and simulations.

The scope of the sources on the World Wide Web is expanding at an overwhelming rate. While schools are educating students to be sophisticated, critical, and effective users of information resources, schools can use Web sites to connect students and staff with high quality, reliable resources. The school Web site can be a jump point to evaluated resources that support the curriculum. Providing relevant resources of excellent quality demonstrates to students what they are expected to find when they search the Web independently. Putting resources online also means that more and more students will have quick and easy access to these carefully selected materials in their own homes on any day around the clock.

Figure 1.4 Payson High School—Mr. Pauley's Site

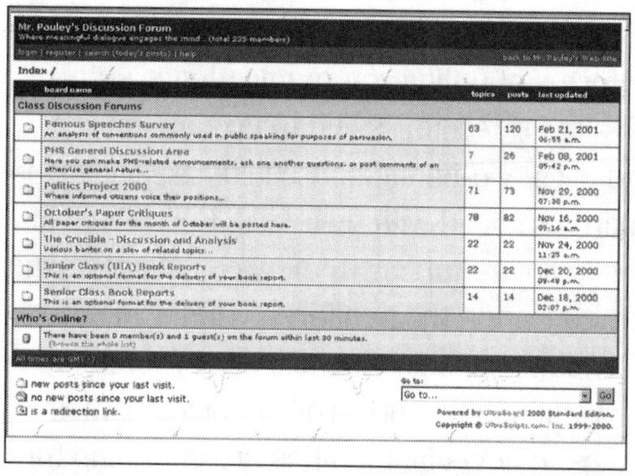

<http://www.phsenglish.com/cgi-bin/UltraBoard/ UltraBoard.cgi>
Mr. Pauley's English classes have the added support of online discussion forums. Students can post their work, get feedback and help, and voice their opinions and concerns. There is also a forum for discussion about topics beyond the scope of the English class forums. *Joe Pauley, Payson High School, Payson, Arizona*

Educators can create spaces on school Web sites to bring students and teachers together outside the classroom. Electronic meeting rooms for private discussions between teachers and students allow students an opportunity for greater privacy, without the inevitable questions from curious peers. Students with health or behavioral issues that do not permit their attending school full time can use the Web version of the classroom to interact with teachers and classmates. This modified classroom can help a student make a gradual transition into attending a classroom full time.

An online meeting room can also be used to bring experts, such as scientists and authors, into the classroom to connect learners to authentic resources and events. Live forums on specific topics often find students who might be less vocal in face-to-face discussions speaking out and participating in the virtual environment. Although many students are already familiar with forms of communication such as e-mail, chat, and instant messaging, most students have not used them for anything but socializing. By bringing these communication spaces into school Web sites and guiding their use, schools are helping teachers and students become more practical users of the technologies for better and more sophisticated communication. Instead of being passive users of information, students become part of the information process as producers and communicators of information.

Gathering and showcasing student projects provides excitement and inspiration for students, parents, and teachers. In recent years, students have increasingly published

Figure 1.5 American Biographies

American Biographies

Welcome
to
American Biography

Eighth grade middle school students wrote these biographies about famous (and infamous) figures in American history. We will be more than happy to correct any historical errors brought to our attention. We are also very interested in your feedback and will try to add any persons you suggest. This page was launched on February 14, 1996, and as time goes by, we will be adding more biographies. Please email   with your comments.

<http://www.gms.ocps.k12.fl.us/biopage/bio.html>
Here's a collection of American Biographies, all written by eighth grade students at Gotha Middle School. This site provides great resources for other students and serves as an excellent example of students contributing to the body of knowledge on the Web.
Eric Lundman, Gotha Middle School, Windermere, Florida

Web pages for personal and school use. At first, when students began to publish on the Web, the ensuing Web site was often the goal and was not viewed as a communication tool. Now, students are being challenged to use Web pages as the presentation method to demonstrate and showcase information that they have learned. Students can develop and expand upon a variety of literacy and higher-level thinking skills as they learn to communicate their understanding to others while practicing evaluation and self-editing. Web pages can be created as group projects. These projects can help students develop critical collaboration skills. In the process, students begin to see how they can actively contribute to the body of human knowledge and to develop a sense of social responsibility. Student-created Web pages provide an excellent opportunity for students to experience firsthand the power of this new global medium and to consider the impact it can have on individual perspectives.

Making these types of resources available to students will help facilitate the development of students' information and technical skills. Information and technology skills are life skills. As educators, we must ensure that children avoid being information-poor and unskilled in an increasingly information-rich and sophisticated society.

▶ ENGAGING EDUCATORS

Educational Web sites can stimulate creative and innovative teaching and learning. Many teachers join students in being motivated and inspired by the resources available through educational Web sites. Collections of links on school Web sites can help teachers in the preparation and rejuvenation of old lessons and in the generation of new lessons. Educators can create Web sites or link to sites that can help them meet their students' individual learning needs. Web sites can be tailor-made to address local curricula or to help students achieve government-mandated standards. These resources can continue to grow each year into compilations of collaborative, localized support materials. Discussion areas on educational Web sites allow teachers to open their classroom walls to the global community. Online collaborations are not limited to buildings or bogged down by

> **FAST FACT**
>
> Some online resources and activities, such as secure forms and discussion areas, require a level of technical expertise and support that is beyond the programming abilities of amateurs.

Figure 1.6 Montgomery County Public Schools Web Site Database

<http://filemaker.mcps.k12.md.us/websites/>
Making use of the ability to interface with databases, Montgomery Public Schools provides visitors with the opportunity to find or suggest educational Web sites. MCPS reviews all submissions before adding them to the database. *David Kreisberg, Montgomery County Public Schools, Rockville, Maryland*

the pace of "snail mail" (a.k.a. postal mail). Web pages to support and enhance specific collaborations can be created as often as needed.

School Web sites are not just learning tools; they are tied in with the very workings of the school itself. Discussion areas allow teachers to connect with other educators for research and support. These areas can also be used to increase local expertise, enhance problem-solving mechanisms, and improve professional relationships. Web sites can be used for developing staff, posting policies, and communicating other internal information. Web sites can facilitate collaboration among staff members from different buildings. Online meetings eliminate travel time and can take place at mutually agreeable times during the school day. Educational Web pages can be used to maintain contact with retirees and to foster their continued involvement in the schools. Secure online forms can replace paper forms. The data collected in this manner are ready to be manipulated. A fringe benefit to this form of communication is the amount of paper saved when information can be e-mailed or posted to mailing lists, bulletin boards, and so forth.

► JUST THE BEGINNING . . .

Educators are just beginning to explore the ways that Web sites can help serve students, parents, communities, and other educators. Once educators have determined how the Web can meet the needs of the particular situation, they are ready to form a vision for the Web site.

Chapter 2

How to Get from Idea to Web Site: Beginning Steps

Now the fun is going to start! But we mustn't dilly! We mustn't dally!...
We have an enormous number of things to do...Good! Everyone ready!
Come on, then! Here we go!

—Roald Dahl

The winners of Willy Wonka's golden tickets in Roald Dahl's *Charlie and the Chocolate Factory* (Knopf, 1964) are faced with a staggering array of things to do at the beginning of their tour. Getting ready to plan a Web site presents an equally staggering array of things to do. This chapter starts a step-by-step overview of the process for planning educational Web pages. This chapter emphasizes questions that can be answered only internally or locally. Corresponding check sheets, worksheets, and other planning sheets are located in **Appendix 1** to assist Web planners and authors in developing their own meaningful and high quality Web sites. The information in this chapter is presented in a linear fashion, but it does not necessarily have to be used that way. Like the Web itself, the process of building Web sites is involved and interconnected. The contents of this chapter are connected to detailed information found throughout this book.

The process of building an educational Web site begins with creating a Web planning team. Web planning teams are strongly recommended for the development of district and school-level Web sites. Departments, grade-level, and teaching teams may also decide that having a Web team will result in a Web site that best meets the needs of the entire group.

◣ WEB PLANNING TEAM

Two heads are better than one. Five or more heads are even better still. When a group consists of diverse planners, the Web planning process benefits from the synergy generated by that group. The involvement of the various stakeholders in the process of developing a vision statement also increases interest in the Web site and its credibility. The process of creating a vision and planning a Web site can also be a public relations tool. Consider inviting interested individuals to represent key groups and to be part of the process. Stakeholders/possible team members may include the following:

1. Teachers
2. Students
3. Administrative staff
4. Technical personnel
5. Librarian/media specialist
6. Support staff
7. Parents
8. Alumni
9. Community members (other educators, organization members, people from business and industry, and so forth)

These stakeholders can become part of a Web planning team that will guide the Web planning process. To prepare them for the process, some training may be helpful. Depending on the backgrounds of team members, they may need basic training on the subjects of Web publishing (an overview of terminology, possibilities, technical considerations, design concepts, vision statements, goals, and so forth).

Develop a communication system for the team. Consider keeping other interested stakeholders informed and involved in the planning process. Communication tools might include meetings, mailing lists, discussion forums, newsletters, or bulletins. For more information on Web planning teams, **see** the section *Creating Web Teams* in **Chapter 6**, *Gathering Resources . . . Just Who Is Needed?* **See also** *District Web Planning Team Information Sheet* and *School Web Planning Team Information* in **Appendix 1**.

◣ WHY, WHO, AND WHAT?

Why create school and educational Web sites? The answer depends on what is to be accomplished and for whom. Once a Web team has been assembled, the members need to start by determining why the site is being created, who is the intended audience, and what the site is to accomplish. These questions need to be answered thoughtfully and clearly. The answers will help to create a vision for the Web site.

Before writing the vision statement, involve representatives from various groups, set goals, identify audiences, determine needs, and research existing Web resources. Although the research involved in creating a vision statement may seem like too much effort for "just" two or three sentences, the information gathered during this process will be a valuable resource that will be revisited throughout the process of creating the Web site.

Why

To get a good start, stop . . . and think about the reason(s) the organization is contemplating creating or updating an educational Web site. Form a general picture of what the Web site is intended to accomplish. What are the underlying goals of the site?

Some of the reasons or goals might be related to the following:

1. Political issues
2. Image or public relations efforts
3. Parent and community involvement, promotions, and communication
4. Educational or student needs
5. Internal organization and communication
6. Generation of revenue

Who

Defining the Web site's **primary audience** goes hand-in-hand with determining reasons for building or revising a Web site. Consider the following regarding the primary audience:

1. Ability levels (reading and comprehension levels)
2. Learning needs (learning styles, curricular content, and so forth).
3. Special needs (personal and technological)
4. Accessibility requirements
5. Cultural sensitivities
6. Community issues
7. Other needs and issues

Although a page may be created for one particular audience, other visitors, or **secondary audiences**, invariably will use the resource unless it is hidden or access is limited through the use of passwords. Primary and secondary audiences might include the following:

1. Alumni
2. Community members
3. Parents
4. Relatives
5. Students
6. Children in other schools
7. Casual surfers
8. Teachers
9. Administrators
10. Other educators

What

While developing a Web site vision, find out what the primary and secondary audiences think is important and what they need. This process can be formal or informal and can be accomplished through the use of tools such as the following:

1. Surveys
2. Focus groups
3. Discussions
4. Casual conversations

Explore potential ways the Web can be molded to meet the needs of the intended audience by gathering ideas and examples of what is possible. Go shopping for ideas. Use the following resources to locate a wide variety of education resources on the Web. Some of these resources are evaluative and list only what they consider to be "the best of the best." Others simply strive to be comprehensive and will list all known resources.

1. Visit other school Web sites.

- *Peter Milbury's Network of School Librarian Web Pages*
  <http://www.school-libraries.net/>
  Milbury has assembled an extensive listing of school, library, professional, and personal Web sites created by school librarians/media specialists.

- *School Libraries on the Web: A Directory*
  <http:// www.sldirectory.com/index.html>
  Created by a school library media specialist from Pennsylvania, this Web site is an impressive directory of school libraries on the Web.

- *Web66: A K–12 World Wide Web Project*
  <http://web66.coled.umn.edu/>
  Web66 is one of the most comprehensive listings of school Web sites from around the world.

- *Yahoo! Education > K–12 > Schools*
  <http://dir.yahoo.com/Education/K_12/Schools/ >
  Yahoo lists thousands of school Web sites.

2. Use these books to find recommended and recognized educational sites.

- Allen C. Benson and Linda M. Fodemski's *Connecting Kids and the Internet: A Handbook for Librarians, Teachers, and Parents Second Edition* (Neal-Schuman, 1999).
  This book discusses a wide variety of recommended Web sites for children.

- Elizabeth Miller's *The Internet Resource Directory for K–12 Teachers and Librarians 2000/2001 Edition* (Libraries Unlimited, 2000). Miller frequently updates this directory of educational Web sites. A number of the sites listed are school Web sites.

- Carol Simpson and Sharron L. McElmeel's *Internet for Schools: A Practical Guide* (Linworth Publishing, Inc., 2000). McElmeel and Simpson list a variety of school and educational Web sites.

3. Check out lists of award-winning sites.

- Education World's *Cool Schools*
  <http://www.educationworld.com/cool_school/index.shtml >

Education World recognizes excellent school Web sites by giving the *Cool Schools* award and provides links to the winners.

- Canada SchoolNet's Site Builder Awards
  <http://www.schoolnet.ca/builders/e/>
  This site highlights the best of Canadian school Web sites.

4 Explore Chapter 3 *Possible Pages . . . What Goes on an Educational Web Site?*

▶ PUT IT IN WRITING . . .

Once possibilities have been explored and decisions about purpose and targeted audiences have been made, it is time to create a vision. The vision statement will become a road map that will guide Web planners and creators through the process of creating a worthwhile Web site. The vision statement will be used to answer questions and determine standards as decisions are made, goals are set, content is created, the site is built, pages are updated, materials are maintained, and results are evaluated. Creating a vision statement is an essential step.

A vision statement will embody the Web site's reason for existing in no more than two or three sentences. The vision statement should also address the purpose and the function of the plan. In terms of the purpose, the vision should address the reason for the site, what it is intended to accomplish, and how the purpose is to be accomplished. The statement should be clear, yet broad enough not to curtail creativity.

The statement should reflect the answers to these questions:

1 What is the site to accomplish?

2 Who are the targeted primary and possibly secondary audiences?

3 What types of pages will be on the site (e.g., e-library, Webquest, teacher resource, and so forth)?

See *Web Site Vision Statement Worksheet* in **Appendix 1**.

IDEAS IN ACTION:

SAMPLE VISION STATEMENT

The Taft Library Media Center Web site is to assist students, faculty, and parents locate and use electronic information resources by providing a user-friendly site with links and information that are selected and written to meet basic information needs and to support curriculum and instruction.

—Taft Library Media Center

QUICK TIP

Individuals creating a simple or even complex individual classroom Web site will go through a simpler process for creating a vision statement than the process for creating a district or school Web site. Teachers creating classroom Web sites are likely to begin with clearly defined reasons for wanting to create a presence on the Web for their classrooms. Even if the planner is simply creating a classroom site, it is still a good idea to take a moment and write down the reason for the Web site in one or two sentences. Keep the statement handy to help prioritize and make decisions about content.

Likewise, creating departmental, team, or grade-level site vision statements does not necessarily call for the level of outside involvement desirable when creating school or district Web pages.

▶ EXPLORING POSSIBLE EDUCATIONAL WEB PAGES AND THEN GETTING DOWN TO BUSINESS: FOUNDATIONS FOR INFORMED DECISION-MAKING

Once the vision statement is created, informed decisions must be made, goals and objectives set, and a time line determined. "Informed" is a key word. Before making decisions, explore the possibilities and limitations of educational Web publishing. Chapter 3, *Possible Pages . . . What Goes on an Educational Web Site?*, looks at an array of possible Web pages. The three chapters that follow address Web publishing policies, copyright, and support personnel. Explore all of these aspects of Web publishing before making detailed plans. Prior to forming a Web planning team, administrators may want to address issues and concerns, such as Web publishing support and policies.

⬛ CHECKING OUT POLICY, COPYRIGHT, SUPPORT, AND TECHNICAL CONSIDERATIONS

Publishing on the Internet raises safety, legal, and other issues. Key to good Web site planning is district Web publishing policies and guidelines that have been developed to support and guide Web publishing. Before a Web planning team makes decisions about goals and objectives, team members must have access to district Web publishing policies and guidelines. Chapter 4, *Blueprints for a Firm Foundation: Publishing Guidelines and Policies,* discusses the development of policies and guidelines. Publishing on the Net in the absence of a district Web publishing policy is essentially publishing without a net for both the Web publishers and the administration. Liability is a realistic concern and possibility. If one does not already exist, a Web publishing policy must be developed before the Web planning team makes decisions. If administrators are uninterested in developing a district Web publishing policy, the best advice to educational Web publishers is to err on the side of extreme caution. **See also** *Publishing Guidelines and Policies Form* in **Appendix 1**.

Caution is also the watchword when dealing with copyright issues on the Web. Web planning teams need to be aware that misconceptions abound about copyright and, in particular, about how copyright applies to Web use and publishing. Awareness of the copyright laws and how they apply to the Web is fundamental information when planning educational Web sites. Chapter 5 covers *Copyright Issues and the Web*. **See also** *Copyright Check Sheet* in **Appendix 1**.

Ideally, a Web planner or planning team will have access to expert advice and information about the technical realities of the situation while decisions are being made. Information about technical support, possibilities, capabilities, limitations, and resources can shape and influence decisions and goals. The technical members of a Web team will provide this type of advice or will know whom to contact to provide answers to these types of questions. A list of resource people can be an invaluable tool for Web planning teams and Web builders. These subjects are covered in Chapter 6, *Gathering Resources . . . Just Who Is Needed?,* and Chapter 7, *Technical Considerations*. **See also** *Web Planning Team Information Sheet, School Web Planning Team Information Sheet, Technical Support Resource List, and Technical Considerations & Constraints Check Sheet* in **Appendix 1**.

Thinking about types of possible educational Web pages and the potential of the Web as discussed in Chapter 3 is exciting and possibly inspiring, but more information is needed to make informed decisions and plans. Chapters 4, 5, 6, and 7 address the nitty-gritty issues of policy, copyright, support, and technical considerations. Once a Web publishing team knows about the possibilities of educational Web publishing, district Web publishing guidelines and policy, how copyright relates to Web publishing, and available support and resources, it is time to begin translating the Web publishing vision into a plan for action. Chapter 8 looks at the process of making decisions, setting goals and objectives, and creating a time line.

Chapter 3

Possible Pages... What Goes on an Educational Web Site?

"Well," said Charlotte, vaguely, "I don't really know. But I'm working on a plan . . . The plan is in its early stages and hasn't completely shaped up yet, but I'm working on it."

—*E. B. White*

➤ CONTENT! CONTENT! CONTENT!

When pioneering "web author" Charlotte of E. B. White's *Charlotte's Web* (Harper & Row, 1952) contemplated her web work, she carefully considered many things she could weave in her web. The possibilities for educational Web sites are mind-boggling and growing rapidly. While looking at and exploring the possibilities, begin to decide how to make a Web vision a reality. This chapter is intended to be a springboard to assist with an exploration of educational Web sites. It will look at fundamental types of educational Web sites and pages. Ideas for possible contents and essential components of Web sites and pages will also be listed.

A vision statement should drive the contents of an educational Web site. Look at this chapter with the vision statement and unique needs of the school's community and educational environment in mind. Be ready to be selective and creative. Remember that content needs to be original. If someone else has already put something on the Web, link to it. No one can anticipate all the ways that the Web will evolve in even the next few years. If the technology for what is desired is not available this month, check back next month. It may be "old news" by then.

Although educators have a built-in audience for educational Web sites, having useful and compelling content is still crucial. The decisions that are made about the contents of a Web site and pages will make the difference between having a Web site that people visit only once or having one to which people return again and again. Rich and meaningful content is a primary factor in making a Web site successful.

▶ BASICS & TYPES

Educational Web pages and sites can be divided into four main categories:

1 INFORMATIVE: These pages are an online compendium of helpful facts and information.

2 CURRICULAR: Designed to be online learning resources, these Web pages may contain links or activities.

3 SHOWCASE: As the name implies, these pages are used to display student work.

4 REVENUE GENERATION: These pages are created to raise monies for educational organizations.

These categories are elastic. A page may have components from more than one category. Whatever the type of Web site or page, there are **essential elements** that should be included. (Beyond these essential elements, the possible contents of school Web pages are virtually limitless, constantly expanding into new territories and dimensions.)

These pages should be on every Web **site**:

1 Links to the district page or school page

2 Information crediting any graphics or any other copyrighted materials used on the site

3 Information page about the Web site and its creation (This might include elements of the vision statement and information about the individual or group responsible for the pages.)

These items should be on every Web **page**:

1 Title

2 Link to the home page

3 Navigational tools or a menu

4 E-mail address for contacting a staff member or the webmaster

5 Copyright statement

6 URL (uniform resource locator) for the page

7 Date the page was created and date of the most recent update

Informative Pages

Informative sites/pages are like online reference books with essential and helpful information about the following:

1 District

2 School

3 Department (Departments could include math, science, language arts, social studies, health [school nurses], library media, technology, art, music, athletic, or other.)

4 Classroom

5 Grade level

6 Team

An informative site/page can introduce and provide useful information about educational programs to parents, students, the community, and others. Look at this type of site/page as an open file cabinet or information rack/display for public access. **See** *Informative Educational Web Pages Planning Sheet* in **Appendix 1**. Given the global nature of this virtual "brochure rack," it is critical to exercise judgment about what should and should not be public information. Consult the district Web publishing policies/guidelines when planning and creating these types of pages. (**See Chapter 4,** *Blueprints for a Firm Foundation: Publishing Guidelines and Policies,* for information about creating Web publishing policies/guidelines.)

The chart on pages 16-17 lists possible components of informative Web pages. Types of Web sites are used to organize the chart. For example, if a component is likely to be found on district level pages, it is checked.

Figure 3.1 St. Michael's School

<http://www.k12.nf.ca/stm/>
All the important information about the school is quickly accessible from this school home page without being cluttered or difficult to find. *Bob Jackman and Barb Leyte, St. Michael's School, Goose Bay, Newfoundland, Canada*

RESOURCE BOX

SAMPLE WEB PAGES THAT INFORM

Boothbay Region High School Alumni Web Site
<http://brhsalum.tsx.org >
Alumni keep in touch through this Web site.

Groveland Elementary School: Practices and Procedures
<http://www.minnetonka.k12.mn.us/grv/practices_&_procedures.htm>
Practices and procedures are spelled out on the Groveland Web site.

Halifax Regional School Board: Documents and Links
<http://www.hrsb.ns.ca/documents/>
Halifax provides a virtual document depot.

Henry Wise Wood Online: Curriculum: English
<http://www.cbe.ab.ca/b836/curriculum/default.htm>
Course listings and descriptions are available online.

Moorhead Elementary School
<http://www.warren.k12.in.us/moorhead/>
Here is a highly visible and clear school calendar.

UTILIZING INFORMATIVE EDUCATIONAL WEB PAGES

	DISTRICT	SCHOOL	DEPARTMENT	GRADE LEVEL	TEAM	CLASSROOM
Contact information	✓	✓	✓	✓	✓	✓
■ directory	✓	✓	✓	✓		
■ individual's school phone numbers	✓	✓	✓	✓	✓	✓
■ staff e-mail addresses	✓	✓	✓	✓	✓	✓
■ fax numbers	✓	✓				
■ who to call for help & when	✓	✓	✓	✓	✓	✓
Mission statement	✓	✓	✓	✓	✓	✓
Letter/greeting from the superintendent principal, teacher, other	✓	✓	✓	✓	✓	✓
Goals & objectives	✓	✓	✓	✓	✓	✓
Strategic or other long-term plans	✓	✓			✓	✓
Locations (maps)*	✓	✓				
Hours	✓	✓				
Pictures of building(s)*	✓	✓	✓			
Information about mandated testing (include overall results for building and/or district)	✓	✓	✓	✓	✓	✓
Accreditation	✓	✓				
District/school history	✓	✓				
Symbols (motto, logo, mascot, other)	✓				✓	
Demographics	✓					
Staff statistics/professional biographies*	✓	✓	✓	✓	✓	✓
Registration procedures and materials (could be printed and returned or sent electronically with a secure system)	✓	✓				
Fees	✓	✓	✓	✓	✓	✓
Supply lists	✓	✓	✓	✓	✓	✓
Menus	✓	✓				
Weather and other emergency procedure information (closings & delays)	✓	✓				
Board meeting agendas and open session minutes	✓					
Committee information and possibly minutes (can be password protected)	✓	✓	✓	✓	✓	
Budget information	✓	✓				
Vendor informaion (shipping and billing procedures)	✓					
Job postings	✓	✓				
Alumni information	✓	✓				
■ reunion information	✓	✓				
■ famous alumni	✓	✓				
■ contact forms	✓	✓				
newsletters—stories and information about what is happening in the district, school, department, classroom	✓	✓	✓	✓	✓	✓
Awards & honors*	✓	✓	✓	✓	✓	✓
Bus route and transportation information*	✓	✓				
Calendar/timeline*	✓	✓	✓	✓	✓	✓
■ school year with holidays & breaks						
■ sports with scores						
■ special events	✓	✓	✓	✓	✓	✓

	DISTRICT	SCHOOL	DEPARTMENT	GRADE LEVEL	TEAM	CLASSROOM
■ field trips	✓	✓	✓	✓	✓	✓
■ units of study			✓	✓	✓	✓
■ assignment due dates			✓	✓	✓	✓
■ testing (including mandated & standardized tests)	✓	✓	✓	✓	✓	✓
Curricula overview	✓	✓	✓	✓	✓	✓
Student handbook	✓	✓				
Policies and procedures	✓	✓	✓	✓	✓	✓
■ dress code	✓	✓				
■ homework		✓	✓	✓	✓	✓
■ discipline	✓	✓	✓	✓	✓	✓
■ attendance	✓	✓				
■ expectations/rules		✓	✓	✓	✓	✓
■ drug policy	✓	✓				
Online grade book (password protected) and final grades (with class ranking & GPA)		✓	✓		✓	✓
Attendance records (password protected)		✓			✓	✓
Information sheets and permission forms for parents (could be printed out and returned or sent electronically with a secure system)		✓	✓		✓	✓
Special services	✓	✓	✓	✓	✓	✓
Special programs	✓	✓	✓	✓	✓	✓
Graduation requirements	✓	✓	✓	✓	✓	
College credit opportunities	✓	✓	✓	✓	✓	
Scholarship information and resources	✓	✓	✓			
Extra curricular activities/school sponsored clubs	✓	✓	✓	✓	✓	✓
Volunteer requests	✓	✓	✓	✓	✓	✓
PTA/PTO information	✓	✓				
Wish lists	✓	✓	✓	✓	✓	✓
Volunteer information	✓	✓	✓	✓	✓	✓
Links to local/community resources and services	✓	✓	✓	✓	✓	✓
Links to parents' resources	✓	✓	✓			
Helpful tips and other original information (i.e. raising readers, homework tips, parenting information)	✓	✓		✓	✓	✓
Educational research findings	✓	✓	✓	✓	✓	✓
Feedback resources for comments, suggestions, other:	✓	✓	✓	✓	✓	✓
■ e-mail	✓	✓	✓	✓	✓	✓
■ forms	✓	✓	✓	✓	✓	✓
■ surveys	✓	✓	✓	✓	✓	✓
■ guest book	✓	✓	✓	✓	✓	✓
■ listserv	✓	✓	✓	✓	✓	✓
■ bulletin board	✓	✓	✓	✓	✓	✓
■ discussion groups				✓	✓	✓
Resource lists/databases (password protected if needed)	✓	✓	✓	✓	✓	✓

Figure 3.2 Northmount School—Once upon a Science Story

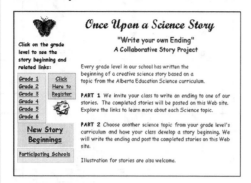

<http://www.epsb.edmonton.ab.ca/schools/
northmount/science/>
Each grade level at Northmount School has written the beginning of a science story. They invite other schools to participate in the project by writing the endings or by writing beginnings for the Northmount students to complete. *Duane Schade, Northmount School, Edmonton, Alberta, Canada*

Curricular Pages

Curricular pages can take a variety of forms and may be directed at a number of audiences. They may be as simple as listings of curricular objectives or as involved as detailed and intricate WebQuests. Web pages such as gateways, e-libraries, portals, or pathfinders direct Web users to other Web sites and can also be curricular. Curricular Web pages may be intended for students, parents, the community, or other educators. Curricular Web pages provide excellent opportunities for educators to reach out to students and to other educators with original, rich resources. Parents are afforded a convenient way to be involved in their child's education when these resources can be accessed easily online. Curricular Web sites do not have to be strictly limited to "The Curriculum." They can enrich and expand upon the curriculum. Given the appeal of using the Web, curricular Web pages can be a great resource for encouraging students to move beyond "just the requirements." **See** *Curricular Pages Planning Sheet* in **Appendix 1**.

Consider the following list of ideas for curricular Web pages and sites:

1 STANDARDS, OBJECTIVES, AND OUTCOMES: Post national, state, and local learner standards, objectives, and outcomes. (Check to see if the learner standards, objectives, or outcomes are under copyright. If necessary, obtain permission before posting them to the Internet.) Show how lessons are aligned to standards. A school system's curricula could be placed on the Web or on a district Intranet, permitting teachers to access curricula from home.

2 ASSIGNMENTS, HANDOUTS, RUBRICS, AND DATES: Place explanations of assignments and online versions of original handouts on the Internet. Consider including any original assessment tools, such as rubrics and check sheets. Share test and due dates.

3 VOCABULARY OR SPELLING LISTS: Make copies of each week's vocabulary or spelling lists available online. (Commercially produced lists are covered by copyright; do not post without obtaining permission.)

4 READING LISTS: Place reading lists online. These can be especially helpful if a student is looking for a book at the public library.

Figure 3.3 Rusk Independent School District—Online Lesson Plans and Homework

<http://www.rusk.esc7.net/karascurrentevents/
onlineplans.html>
Rusk high school and junior high teachers log their class activities and homework into a database. The school Web site provides access to the database and is searchable by teacher or date. Students and parents can always check to see what happened during class and what homework was assigned. *Kara Bowling, Rusk Independent School District, Rusk, Texas*

5 PATHFINDERS: Create and place multimedia pathfinders on educational Web pages. Pathfinders direct users to a variety of recommended resources on a specific topic. Strategies for finding and using resources are integral parts of pathfinders.

6 PROJECT PAGE: Have a flexible page with recommended links and assignment directions that can be updated as needed. A project page archive can house past projects for future use and for use by other educators.

7 SCAVENGER HUNTS: Treat students to online scavenger hunts via the Internet. Design online scavenger hunts so that students must use one or more specific Web sites for their answers. Another option is to have students improve their search skills by searching for answers with online search engines and directories.

Figure 3.4 F.V. Evans Elementary School—Create a State Project

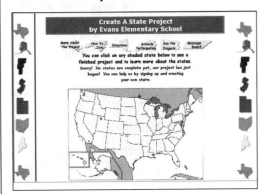

<http://www.evesham.k12.nj.us/evans/states/states.htm>

These elementary school students invited other schools from around the United States to participate with them in this collaborative project. *Karen Biddinger, F.V. Evans Elementary School, Marlton, New Jersey*

8 FACT PAGE OR ARTICLE: Provide students with an original, online fact page to support instruction. The fact page could be written in the form of an online article.

9 TUTORIAL: Ready for a challenge? Consider creating an interactive tutorial or a simulation. A tutorial will teach a topic step-by-step. An interactive tutorial will give students immediate feedback.

10 SIMULATION: Create a virtual situation that emulates a real-life experience.

11 VIRTUAL TOUR OR MUSEUM: Have students tour a museum or other special place by creating a virtual experience on the Web. Use digital versions of photos, documents, videos, sound recordings, and other primary source materials to create the tour/museum.

12 PRACTICE TESTS: Help students prepare for tests by placing practice tests online. Practice tests can be made with online forms and can be password protected. Teachers can use the practice test results to help plan review sessions.

13 PUZZLES: Stimulate student interest by developing online educational puzzles.

14 GATEWAYS/E-LIBRARIES/PORTALS/HOT LINKS: Guide students with a list of links to selected resources by creating a gateway page to curriculum-related links. The links can include helpful sites for homework and references. Always organize and annotate the lists. Gateways are types of online libraries that offer organized access to recommended Web sites.

Figure 3.5 Alvirne High School—AP Calculus Problem of the Week

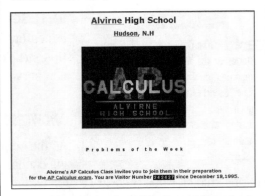

<http://www.seresc.k12.nh.us/www/alvirne.html>

Students needing help with calculus or preparing for calculus exams have a gold mine of resources on this page. Problems of the week, exam information, and archives of problems with solutions create a valuable, specialized, resource page for students. *Sandra Ray, Alvirne High School, Hudson, New Hampshire*

SAMPLE WEB PAGES FOR CURRICULAR SUPPORT

Banded Peak School: Teaching and Learning with Technology
<http://www.rockyview.ab.ca/bpeak/research/tlt/tlt.html>
   Banded Peak schoolteachers share instructional resources online.

Marshfield High School: Accelerated Reader Lists of Quizzes
<http://www.marshfield.coos-bay.k12.or.us/library/accelerated_reader_lists_of_quiz.htm>
   Marshfield makes the AR quiz lists available on this Web site.

Nueva Library: Choose the Best Search for your Information Need
<http://nuevaschool.org/~debbie/library/research/adviceengine.html>
   Nueva provides research guidance for students selecting search tools.

Oradell Public School: How to Compile a Bibliography
<http://www.intac.com/~aroldi/biblio.html>
   The Oradell Web site helps elementary students cite resources.

Rios Elementary School: Standards
<http://www.joelson.addr.com/standards.htm>
   State content standards are communicated on the Rios site.

---

14 WEBQUESTS/RESEARCH INVESTIGATIONS: Create WebQuests (a.k.a. research investigations) to facilitate inquiry-based activities. Use WebQuests to take students through the process of gathering and using information to solve problems.

15 COLLABORATIONS: Curricular Web pages can be collaboration tools. Whether between classmates, classes in the same building, classes in the same region, or classes from different parts of the world, educational Web sites can be used to invite, structure, facilitate, house, and archive online collaborations.

16 LESSONS, TIPS, AND ARTICLES: Share expertise with other educators by using the Web to archive original lessons, tips, articles, and other resources. An educational Web site can serve as a database.

Showcase Pages

As the emphasis on authentic inquiry and project-based learning continues to grow, the Web offers an exciting avenue for sharing student work. Student-created writing, artwork, multimedia presentations, and Web sites can be posted to highlight student work and to provide additional information resources to Web users. Showcasing student work is much more than a way to motivate students and to help them share what they have learned and accomplished—it is a public relations tool that will attract visitors to an educational Web site. More important, it will help others understand what students and educators are doing and learning in their school. It can help reinforce an image of the school as a technologically sophisticated, innovative, and progressive environment with high standards and exciting programs. One educational webmaster received the following comment from a visitor who discovered her school site during a search with the Google search engine <http://www.google.com>: "Congratulations! You must be a very good school."

Showcasing student work can also be used as a learning tool. When students become producers of information for a larger audience, process and quality become more meaningful to students. The need for quality, accuracy, and originality takes on greater importance. As producers of artistic and information products, students and their parents/guardians will have to give permission before student works can be posted online. This step in showcasing student work personalizes the concepts behind protecting the rights of creators of materials and reinforces why they need to respect the intellectual property rights of others. Ironically, it is inadvisable to post personal information about students, such as names (see **Chapter 4**, *Blueprints for a Firm Foundation: Publishing Guidelines and Policies*). Check with school Web publishing policies/guidelines for permissible ways to identify and credit student work.

Figure 3.6 Mount Pleasant—Ancient Images

<http://www.ancientimages.org/>
Through this unique project, fourth grade students learned about not only an important topic but also real-life lessons in business. Commissioned specifically to do the project, each student signed a contract and received a check for $10 once the project was completed. *Beth Smithson, Art Teacher, Mt. Pleasant Elementary School, Mount Pleasant, North Carolina*

RESOURCE BOX

SAMPLE PAGES SHOWCASING STUDENT WORK

Escondido Union School District: California Mission Internet Trail
<http://www.escusd.k12.ca.us/mission_trail/MissionTrail.html>
The heritage of the California Missions is preserved and shared on this site.

Mount Baker Secondary School: Joseph Creek
<http://www.mbaker.com/projects/josephcreek/home.htm>
Students share what they have learned about Joseph Creek.

Newtonite Online
<http://www.tiac.net/users/newtonit/>
Read current and past issues of this student newspaper online.

Palmerston District Primary Schools: Namadgi's Healthy Bodies Site
<http://www.palmdps.act.edu.au/Body/healthy_bodies.htm>
Students share health information.

University Park Elementary School: Microcopium
<http://www.northstar.k12.ak.us/schools/upk/microcopium.html>
This site spotlights a host of student projects.

Student products such as artwork, poetry, compositions, articles, newsletters, newspapers, reports, multimedia presentations (make certain that copyrights are not violated), and Web sites can be showcased on the Web. Online collaborations can showcase student work. Use the Web to create an online student portfolio (may need password protection) or class portfolio highlighting a year's work. Another way to showcase student work is to involve students in creating and maintaining the school's Web site. Students can be vital members of school Web teams. **See** *Showcase Pages Planning Sheet* in **Appendix 1**.

Revenue Generation Pages: A New Dimension of Educational Web Sites

An additional option that is gaining popularity is the ability to raise funds via the school Web site. The ease of building Web pages, combined with the number of opportunities for partnering with various commercial entities across the Web, has created a new door for schools in their quest for much-needed funds. Fund raising on a school Web site broadens the reach of the school. Cristine Santo, in her article "Goodbye Bake Sales" (*Family PC,* October 1999), notes, "The good news about these programs is they're safe for kids (no door-to-door sales, no handling of cash); non-fattening for parents; and extract money from far-flung friends, relatives and strangers, rather than the same pool of generous, local souls." Schools can use a number of methods to raise funds through the school Web site. Before becoming involved in any fund-raising activities, schools must ensure that the school and district Web publishing guidelines permit this type of usage. These four methods require minimal knowledge about building Web pages:

1 ONLINE AUCTIONS allow schools to gather items and auction them to online visitors. To create an auction, schools register with the auction site, list the items they have to offer, and promote the auction to friends, relatives, or the community. The auction site handles the secure financial transactions and promotes the auction through its own advertising network in exchange for a percentage of the proceeds.

2 AFFILIATE PROGRAMS work a bit differently. A school registers as an affiliate with a commercial vendor, creates special links from the school Web site to products at the vendor's site, and receives a commission for any of the products purchased by someone who follows the link from the school site. Two of the best known of these programs are through Amazon.com <www.amazon.com> and Barnes and Noble <www.barnesandnoble.com> for buying books online—natural partners for school library Web sites. It makes sense to provide educational products and services such as books, software, hardware, or online courses through a school Web site. In many ways, adding well-chosen affiliate programs to a school Web site can benefit the community.

Figure 3.7 Buckman School—Dr. King Timeline

<http://www.pps.k12.or.us/district/depts/itss/buckman/time line/kingframe.html>

One of a number of great K–3 projects from Buckman School, this time line contains student artwork depicting the life of Martin Luther King, Jr. *Tim Lauer, Instructional Technology, Portland Public Schools, Portland, Oregon*

3 **SHOP-TO-GIVE PROGRAMS** go a step further than affiliate programs. Instead of choosing individual vendors, the school works with "online shopping malls" containing a full range of products and services. As a member of the program, the school benefits from visitors shopping online in the same manner as they do with affiliate programs. The difference is that the malls may contain products that are not related to education, such as clothing, furniture, cookware, and almost anything else one can name. With online shopping increasing in popularity, shop-to-give programs provide parents and community members the chance to donate to the school in the process.

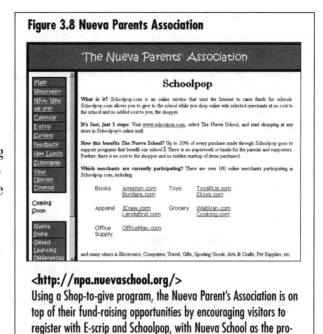

Figure 3.8 Nueva Parents Association

<http://npa.nuevaschool.org/>
Using a Shop-to-give program, the Nueva Parent's Association is on top of their fund-raising opportunities by encouraging visitors to register with E-scrip and Schoolpop, with Nueva School as the program recipient.

4 **ONLINE CHARITY PROGRAMS** are usually limited to nonprofit organizations. Although some schools may not be able to participate, some of the groups associated with the school (parent groups, band clubs, and so forth) may. The organization registers with the online charity site, then creates a special donation page on the local site. The local donation page is used with the charity site to accept donations. In this way, parents, relatives, and community members can donate online directly to the school or club. The charity site handles the secure e-commerce transactions and produces tax receipts in exchange for a percentage of the donations or a small fee.

The key to making any of these fund-raising possibilities work is choosing programs that are appropriate for your school, district, and community and then marketing them properly. Schools will have greater success by promoting the programs as useful services and a way to help the school rather than simply as a way to buy online. "Online shopping isn't likely to replace other fund raising soon, but your school can benefit by using the Internet, as long as you put some work into the marketing." (Seydel, Angela. "Fund-Raising While You Shop: A Look at Fund-Raising Sites on the Internet." *Multimedia Schools,* September 2000). **See** *Revenue Generation Pages Planning Sheet* in **Appendix 1**.

▶ IDEAS IN ACTION: PULLING IT ALL TOGETHER

A single educational Web site can easily combine elements of *informative, curricular, showcase,* and *fund-raising* Web sites. Look for ready-to-use versions of the *Informative Educational Web Pages*, *Curricular Pages*, *Showcase Pages*, and *Revenue Generation Pages* planning sheets in **Appendix 1**.

The planning sheets on pages 26-29 show how a Web site might have aspects of all four types of pages. Each sheet has a priority column that can help determine which parts of the Web site need to be tackled and put into place first and which portions can wait. The process of prioritizing content can be helpful on several levels. First, setting priorities helps the Web planner(s) break the process into manageable steps. Second, the planning sheet gives the Web site designer a notion of what will be added at a later date so that that person can make the site's initial design flexible to accommodate the future additions. Third, by starting small, the Web worker(s) will have a chance to evaluate the usability and effectiveness of the site while it is easier to revise and manage. Before additional content is added, adjustments can be made more easily to the existing site, and the priorities themselves may be adjusted.

For the following planning sheets, note that the number of items checked would result in an extremely ambitious Web project. These sheets are intended to serve as samples that indicate possible contents that might be found on a school Web site.

A school Web site with a combination of informative, curricular, and showcase contents can be a resource for students, parents, teachers, and the community. It can be available on the Internet 24 hours a day, seven days a week. It can be an office, a library media center, a classroom, a teacher's lounge, or a handbook—and it never closes.

RESOURCE BOX

FUND-RAISING LINKS

4Charity
<http://www.4charity.com/nonprofit/services/donation/>
4Charity provides a variety of Web-based services to help nonprofit organizations. Web-based services include Web design, volunteer coordination, direct donation services, greeting cards, and event registration.

CauseLink
<http://www.causelink.com/>
This site "provides complete auction services and online fund-raising solutions to the nonprofit community."

Charity.ca
<http://www.charity.ca>
This online Canadian organization is dedicated to helping charities with fund raising and awareness.

Commission Junction
<http://www.cj.com/>
This affiliate network provides access to and services for a large collection of affiliate programs.

eBay
<http://www.ebay.com>
This "person-to-person online trading community" allows users to buy and sell. In addition, eBay helps nonprofit organizations auction items for the purpose of raising funds.

iGive
<http://www.igive.com>
iGive is an online shopping service that donates a percentage of each purchase to a charity of one's choice.

LinkShare
<http://www.linkshare.com/>
This free affiliate network provides resources and information about affiliate programs and obtains, tracks, and issues payment to members in the network.

rSchool.com
<http://www.rschool.com>
This online education resource center includes information on fund raising.

School Cash
<http://www.schoolcash.com/>
School Cash shop is an online service that donates up to 25% of each purchase to the school of one's choice.

SchoolPop

<http://schoolpop.com/>

This online shopping service donates up to 20% of each purchase to the school of your choice. It includes in-store and catalog shopping in its donation program.

Shop for School

<http://shopforschool.com/>

This online shopping service donates up to 40% of purchases to the school of one's choice. Only online purchases qualify for donation.

WebCharity.com

<http://www.webcharity.com/>

This free, nonprofit organization facilitates online auctions for charities.

Yahoo Auctions

<http://auctions.yahoo.com/>

Yahoo hosts this online public auction.

INFORMATIVE EDUCATIONAL WEB PAGES PLANNING SHEET

PRIORITY		NOTES:
1	Contact information*	✓ School phone #'s. Web Master's e-mail
1	■ Directory	
3	■ individual's school phone numbers	
1	■ staff e-mail address	✓ check district policy & then with staff members to see if they wish to have name & e-mail included
3	■ fax numbers	✓ check to see if this is permitted
2	■ who to call for help and when	✓ could list hours; check to see if this is permitted
1	Mission and/or vision statement	✓ put on administrative page
1	Letter/greeting from the superintendent, principal, teacher, others	✓ note from principal
2	Goals & objectives	✓ general statement about school goals & objectives
1	Strategies or other long-term plans	✓ put on administrative page
	Locations (maps)*	
	Hours*	
1	Pictures of building(s)	✓ Keep small on opening page
1	Information about mandated testing	✓ Include on "what we are learning" page
1	Accreditation	✓ put on administrative page
2	District/school history	✓ check with historical society
1	Symbols (motto, logo, mascot, other)	✓ small version on each page
1	Demographics	✓ stats re: education of faculty on faculty page, i.e., % with Masters degrees
1	Staff statistics/professional biographies*	✓ obtain written release & check district policies first
1	Registration procedures and materials	✓ enrollment info on "contacting school" page
	Fees	
3	Supply lists	✓ at the beginning of the year. have a welcome back page
	Menus	
1	Weather and other emergency procedure information	✓ put weather link to district page on front page
	Board meeting agendas and open session minutes Committee information and possibly minutes	
	Budget information	
	Vendor information	
	Job postings	
3	Alumni information	✓ see if alumni are interested
	■ reunion information	✓ see if alumni are interested
	■ famous alumni	
1	■ contact forms	✓ have place to check if alumni in guest book
2	Newsletter—stories and information about what is happening in the district, school, department, classrooms	✓ publish staff newsletter online. It can be password protected/secure ✓ how about school/parent newsletter? Check policy and tech support
	Awards & honors*	
	Bus route/transportation information*	
	Calendar/time line*	
1	■ school year with holidays & breaks	✓ combination event & calendar page
1/2	■ sports with scores	✓ start with sports schedule...second phase include scores
1	■ special events	✓ combination event & calendar page
	■ field trips	✓ combination event & calendar page
2	■ units of study	✓ involve teachers in planning grade-level calendar for next year. Start tracking units now.
2	■ assignment due dates	✓ This could be included on the "major units" page.

INFORMATIVE EDUCATIONAL WEB PAGES PLANNING SHEET continued

PRIORITY		NOTES:
1/2	■ testing	✓ put state testing dates on combination event & calendar page–highlight
2	Curriculum overview	general curriculum overview for each grade level on the instructional program–"What we are Learning" page
1	Student handbook	✓ handbook page
1	Policies and procedures	✓ handbook page
	■ dress code	✓ handbook page
	■ homework	✓ handbook page
	■ discipline	✓ handbook page
	■ attendance	✓ handbook page
2	■ expectations/rules	✓ handbook page
	■ drug policy	✓ handbook page
3	Online grade book and final grades	✓ check on needed software & support. Can we do this? What do we need?
	Attendance records	
1	Information sheets and permission forms for parents	✓ A printable online version of the district's AUO form that can be printed, filled out, and returned. ✓ A printable online of field trip forms
1	Special services	✓ list
2	Special programs	✓ talented & gifted, music groups and activities, work study, and so forth–should each have own page
	Graduation requirements	
	College credit opportunities	
	Scholarship information and resources	
2	Extracurricular activities/school-sponsored clubs ask them to start brainstorming how they could utilize the Web	✓ drama club, Web Masters club, service groups, and so forth
2	Volunteer requests	✓ explain the types of jobs to be done & information on how to volunteer
1	PTA/PTO information	✓ list materials donated by PTA with a "thank you!"
1	Wish lists materials & equipment	
2	Volunteer information	✓ jobs listed & described
1	Links to local resources and services	✓ Include Internet use and safety information
2	Links to parenting resources	✓ Include Internet use and safety information
2	Helpful tips and other original information	✓ raising readers, homework help, tech troubleshooting, tech shortcuts, building Web pages
3	Educational research findings	✓ workshop handouts and materials
	Feedback resources for comments, suggestions, other	
1	■ e-mail	✓ Webmaster & school e-mail address
2	■ forms	✓ If possible, secure forms for faculty to request materials from the district teaching collection
3	■ surveys	✓ How can we help you?
1	■ guest book	✓ have place to check if alumni
	■ listserv	
2	■ bulletin board	Check to see if resources are available.
	■ discussion groups	
3	Resource lists/databases	✓ Accelerated Reader–check to see if can be supported
	Other	
	Other	
	Other	

*Look at safety considerations/district Web publishing policy before posting this kind of information.

CURRICULAR EDUCATIONAL WEB PAGES PLANNING SHEET

PRIORITY		NOTES:
1	Standards, objectives, and outcomes	✓ Statement that lessons are correlated to stat learner outcomes and the local curriculum on "what we are learning" page
2	Assignments, handouts, rubrics, check sheets, tests, and due date	✓ Post basic project rubrics, due dates, handouts
	Vocabulary and/or spelling lists	
3	Reading lists	✓ summer reading
2	Pathfinders	✓ do pathfinder training with teachers & have them develop
1	Project page	✓ collaboration project resource–responsibility of librarian
3	Scavenger hunts	✓ train teachers to create scavenger hunts
2	Fact page or article	✓ copyright information
1	Tutorial	✓ Internet use. Web site evaluation, citing sources, using primary source guidelines
3	Stimulation	✓ need to see if can be supported & then provide training to teaching staff
1	Virtual tour or museum	✓ tour of community
3	Practice test	✓ check copyright issues
1	Puzzles	✓ curriculum driven–organized by discipline, teacher resources, general reference tools, database links, home work help links, search resources, search engine links
2	Gateway/e-library/portals/hot links	✓ curriculum driven–organized by discipline, teacher resources, general reference tools, databaselinks, homework help links, search engine links, and so forth–librarian responsible
2	Webquests/research investigation	✓ do WebQuest training with teachers & have them develop
3	Collaborative projects	✓ goal–one with other school in district by the end of year 3
3	Educational lesson archive	✓ Start teachers thinking about this now!
3	Educational tips	✓ create citing source page
	Educational articles	

*Look at safety considerations/district Web publishing policy before posting this kind of information.

SHOWCASE PAGES PLANNING SHEET

Reminder: When posting student works, check and follow policy before using student names. Have and use copyright release form.

WORK TO SHOWCASE:

PRIORITY		NOTES:
1	Artwork	✔ Art club page
1	Poetry	✔ Writer's Block page
1	Composition/prose	✔ Writer's Block page
	Article*	
2	Newsletters*	✔ check for ideas on how to avoid use of personal information or if it can be made secure
2	Newspapers*	✔ check for ideas on how to avoid use of personal information or if it can be made secure
	Reports	
2	Multimedia presentations	✔ annual Animal HyperStudio projects–check copyright issues
1	Web sites	✔ involve students with creating virtual tour of the community
3	Collaborative projects	✔ showcase resulting work from district collaboration online
	Student portfolio	
3	Class portfolio	✔ discuss possibility with teachers
	Other	
	Other	
	Other	

*Look at safety considerations/district Web publishing policy before posting this kind of information.

REVENUE GENERATION PAGES

PRIORITY		NOTES:
1	Online auctions	
2	Affiliate programs	✔ become an Amazon affiliate–check district policy first!
	Online charity programs	
	Other	
	Other	

*Look at safety considerations/district Web publishing policy before posting this kind of information.

Blueprints for a Firm Foundation: Publishing Guidelines and Policies

I don't mind your thinking slowly; I mind your publishing faster
than you think.

—*Wolfgang Pauli, Swiss Physicist*

Anyone with access to a computer and the Internet can now publish almost whatever
they want on the Web. When it comes to school Web sites, clear, effective publishing
guidelines and policies are needed that will keep school Web authors working within
specific boundaries so they do not "publish faster than they think."

What are publishing guidelines and policies? If the Internet is viewed as an Information
Superhighway, publishing guidelines and policies are the local "rules of the road." **Guidelines** allow
for bending the rules when necessary. Publishing **policies,** on the other hand, are strict regulations.

Guidelines include suggestions and expectations that encourage school Web authors to
think critically and to allow them to make decisions surrounding particular aspects of their
work. Possible suggestions include statements such as "Keep download times within reasonable limits." Reasonable, in this case, depends upon the project or page and is calculated with
additional variables, such as whether the pages will be viewed internally only or will be available globally across the Web. The expectations contain specific parameters and statements
such as "Post a contact e-mail at the bottom of every page." It is not a suggestion; it is an
expectation, but not critical enough to be "policy."

Publishing policies are not flexible. They are the rules that are not to be bent or broken. Policies are critical, essential regulations that absolutely must be followed—or the school, district, staff, or students could face serious consequences. Policies usually communicate legal and safety issues. They consist of items such as "All student work must be accompanied by a signed release form." Both publishing guidelines and policies are found in documents guiding school Web publishing.

Why are publishing guidelines and policies necessary? They provide direction to Web authors so that authors build the type of site the school or district wants and expects—not only in the way the site looks and functions but also in how it represents the students, staff, school, or district. Web publishing guidelines and policies remind Web authors to consider issues surrounding copyright, intellectual property, and other legal issues. Good publishing guidelines and policies will also include, or link to, other district documents such as Acceptable Internet Use or Network Access Policies, if available. Without guidelines, anything goes, and schools can soon find themselves snarled in all kinds of issues, possibly even lawsuits.

Publishing guidelines and policies help schools manage the following:

1 CONSISTENCY: Publishing guidelines and policies communicate a standardized design, layout, and navigation, as well as standardized construction techniques and requirements, to all Web authors. This is essential so that viewers know they have not left the site as they move from page to page. Consistency also provides a level of professionalism that is important to the marketing aspect of school Web sites. With parents now "shopping" for schools, the school Web site must provide the best possible face for the school.

2 MAINTENANCE: Clear guidelines for writing can help authors avoid needless rewrites. Web authors know in advance what is not permitted and the level of writing that is expected. Publishing guidelines can help ease compatibility issues as administrators stitch the work of many authors into a unified site. Guidelines can remind Web administrators to follow a suggested maintenance schedule. The goal of these guidelines is to ensure that the school Web site provides valuable, high quality information for visitors, functions effectively, and stays current.

3 SAFETY AND LIABILITY: These guidelines and policies provide parameters for Web authors that protect students, staff, the school, and the district. Guidelines surrounding safety issues also help students consider how to be responsible, ethical citizens and how to represent themselves and others to the world. These guidelines and policies include how to handle copyright issues, acknowledge sources of information, and protect personal privacy. Schools and districts demonstrate awareness of and attention to legal issues by communicating specific publishing policies to Web authors. Guidelines and polices clarify Web issues related to accountability and contact information. Compliance with clearly defined safety and liability guidelines and policies can help schools avoid issues, promote a safe Web environment, and create a buffer for challenges to content.

No one set of guidelines works for every school or district—one size *doesn't* fit all. Some school districts create different publishing guidelines for varying levels of the organization—one set for the district level, one for departments and schools, and still another for classroom pages. Although some elements are common to all environments, each environment is unique; specifics of the guidelines will vary between levels, schools, and districts. Although the guidelines and policies may vary between levels of the organization, the school or district always has the right to remove anything it deems inappropriate.

> **QUICK TIP**
>
> The Hillsboro School District in Oregon has created different guidelines for varying levels of its organization. Available at <http://www.hsd.k12.or.us/district/technology/webpublish.htm#DIFFER>

Many guidelines and policies develop from the decisions by school and district Web teams. The purpose of publishing guidelines and policies is to "enshrine" those decisions into an official document. This document becomes a communication tool that guides school and district Web authors, and should be easily accessible to anyone who is creating pages for the site. (Guidelines are usually published on the school or district Web site.) **See** *Publishing Guidelines and Policies Check Sheet* in **Appendix 1**.

➤ DESIGN AND TECHNICAL GUIDELINES

Design and technical guidelines are necessary for designing, building, and working on school Web pages, just as they are necessary for other businesses. Design guidelines cover such items as the use of colors, fonts, white space, navigation, and graphics. Most Web design books will cover common Web design principles, and these principles apply, with little exception, to schools. Technical guidelines cover such items as the type of files that can be used on the site, file naming conventions, and restrictions on the size of the files. Chapter 9, *What Makes a Well-Designed Educational Web Site?,* includes many design and construction elements that can become part of the school or district guidelines. Chapter 7, *Technical Considerations,* provides an overview of the many technical issues that will need to be addressed. Some of these technical considerations will also become part of the publishing guidelines.

Some of the most common design and technical guidelines include or address the following:

1. Consistent layout and colors for all pages (except for student work)
2. The same font styles and families throughout the site
3. Navigation tools in the same place on every page
4. Link to main sections of the site from each page
5. Contact information on every page
6. Download time kept to a minimum on all pages
7. A check for pages with different browsers, monitors, and platforms
8. Text alternatives to images for accessibility
9. Text links with image maps and linked graphics
10. Restrictions on file types that can be used

The discussion on pages 66–71 addresses why some of the items on the preceding list are included in design and technical guidelines.

Consistency

Define how information should appear in page headers or footers. This not only maintains consistency but also ensures that none of the pages becomes an "orphan"—a page without "parents." Common footers designate ownership and help with navigation in case the visitor finds the page through a search tool rather than through the home page on the site. Here are examples of requirements for headers and footers:

1. Links required to specific pages on the site (home, primary pages, or both)
2. Details about copyright format (word, symbol, or both)
3. Author and contact formats (initials, first name only, e-mail only, and so forth)
4. date formats (creation date, revision date, or both)

The guidelines need to specify whether particular font styles, sizes, or colors should be used in particular sections of the site. If the same font should be in the Web version and print versions of the school newsletter, the Web authors need to know. The guidelines can maintain consistency between publications or departments, and will improve the readability on the site.

The guidelines should state any restrictions surrounding the use, placement, or modification of banners or logos that are owned by the school. This helps maintain a consistent image associated with the school and keeps tampering with the image in check. Schools and districts can define the following attributes of logos and banners:

1. Which logos or banners can be used
2. Restrictions as to location on the page
3. Text that should be attached to them
4. Changes to specific logos and banners that are/are not allowed

Minimizing Download Times

Jamie Mackenzie, in his 1997 article "Home Sweet Home: Creating WWW Pages That Deliver" <http://www.fno.org/homesweet.html>, made a suggestion to provide limits on the physical dimensions of images submitted by students. Although this is one way to keep the download time for pages to a minimum, file size makes the biggest difference. The number of images on a page also impacts download time. Additional recommendations include the following:

1. Set a maximum file size.
2. Use thumbnails for images over a specific file size.
3. List the file size in text beside all multimedia clips.
4. Limit the number of graphics per page or section.
5. Designate specific graphics that can be used repeatedly.

Accessibility Requirements

Accessibility primarily refers to making Web content usable by people with disabilities. Design guidelines should give direction about accessibility requirements for school Web sites. Accessibility guidelines can range from designating which Web browser software should be able to read the pages, to ensuring that the site can be read by those with visual and auditory impairments, physical disabilities, or even those who are cognitively or language challenged. Assistive technologies enable individuals with disabilities to use the Web and can be added with a few simple Web construction practices.

In the United States, incorporating accessibility features into school Web sites has become a pressing issue. *A Guide to Disability Rights Laws* < http://www.usdoj.gov/crt/ada/cguide.htm#anchor62335> (U.S. Department of Justice, May 2000) notes that Title II of the Americans with Disabilities Act "requires that State and local governments give people with disabilities an equal opportunity to benefit from all of their programs, services, and activities (e.g., public education, employment, transportation, recreation, health care, social services, courts, voting, and town meetings)." Joe Wheaton, Associate Professor at The Ohio State University, notes that this requirement extends to educational institutions' (See his article "Web Page Accessibility: A Forgotten Requirement for Distance Education" *Rehabilitation Education,* Summer 2001 [in press] available at < *http://www.osu.edu/grants/dpg/wheaton_%20et_%20al_2000.html>.)* Under this Act, schools and districts that receive government funding are

> **FAST FACT**
>
> Bobby is a Web resource that will check pages for accessibility and provide a detailed report for free. Bobby differentiates between levels of accessibility. Available at <http://www.cast.org/bobby/>

required to be accessible to users with disabilities. Accessibility needs to address disabilities such as color blindness, hearing impairments, deafness, low vision, blindness, speech impairments, cognitive disabilities, neurological disabilities, motor impairments, and physical disabilities. If educational Web sites are not accessible, the funding may be compromised. Although access is not an issue in Canada at the time of this writing, Canadian legislation could easily follow suit. Accessibility guidelines and information from the Government of Canada are available at <http://www.psc-cfp.gc.ca/eepmppmpee/ programoverview/eeerc_2_e.htm>.

Schools and school districts need to set goals for accessibility, decide which features must be included on the site, and communicate those standards to authors by means of the guidelines. Chapter 9, *What Makes a Well-Designed Educational Web Site?,* has information about making Web sites accessible.

> **"Due to the current state of Web technology, Web sites cannot be made totally accessible. The goal is to make Web sites as accessible as possible by placing the most emphasis on content and meaning, rather than [on] style and glitter."**
>
> University of Wisconsin-Madison, *Accessibility Guidelines for WWW Home Pages*
> <http://www.wisc.edu/wiscinfo/policy/guidelines.html>

Restricting File Types

Students are becoming adept at creating scripts and programs, yet it is up to the school to dictate what can be loaded on the server (Java, JavaScript, CGIs, DHTML, and so forth). Because some scripts and programs can pose a security risk, whoever is uploading should always know what the files are for before putting them on the Web site.

▶ CONTENT GUIDELINES

A common directive of educational Web pages is that they be curriculum driven. Chapter 3, *Possible Pages: What Goes on an Educational Web Site?,* suggests many items that could reasonably appear on a school Web site. However, content guidelines explain the type of materials the school *allows* on the site. The guidelines provide direction on the quality of writing expected and retention periods that apply. Policies or guidelines surrounding the representation of commercial organizations or fund-raising activities through the school Web site also fall into this category.

In addition to having guidelines that recommend types of content, schools may have policies that prohibit some content. Some schools allow external organizations to have pages on the Web site (e.g., parent action groups, Friends of the Library, literacy groups), while other schools do not. Districts that do allow these external uses of the school Web site must be prepared to include direction in their publishing guidelines and policies regarding what information can appear on the pages. It is also wise to require that the external pages include a disclaimer of some kind that informs visitors of the neutral position of the school or district regarding the content of the external pages.

> **QUICK TIP**
>
> E-libraries, link libraries, portals, or gateways are collections of resource links that support the curriculum or provide access to topics of interest to staff or students. It is important not only to apply sound evaluation criteria during the selection of sites but also to consult the library's collection development policy. Just because it is easy and inexpensive to create links does not mean it is worthwhile. Not every donated book is appropriate for a library, and neither is every free link. Be sure to involve library staff in the creation of these link libraries.

> **QUICK TIP**
>
> Districts that allow external organizations to have pages on the school or district Web site must have a clear set of criteria regarding the type of organizations they will allow. Issues can arise when schools allow one group, but not another, to have representation.

"Do not use busy backgrounds. Even if the text shows up clearly on the background, it can be difficult for people to read if there is too much "noise." Plain white is always a safe choice."

Dennis-Yarmouth Regional School District, *Suggested Guidelines for School, Department, and Classroom Web Pages* <http://www.dy-regional.k12.ma.us/pdf/schoolwebpages.pdf>

"Graphics may be composed in any program but must be converted to GIF or JPEG/JPG format. PNG graphics will be served correctly but may not be supported by client browsers at this time."

Fairbanks North Star Borough School District, *Web Publishing Standards and Guidelines* <http://www.northstar.k12.ak.us/guides/standards.html>

"Due to limited storage space and varying network speeds, it is recommended that file sizes should be kept under 50 Kilobytes. In rare cases, where larger file sizes are required, please inform users by making a note on referring documents."

Davis School District Internet/Intranet Publishing Guidelines <http://www.davis.k12.ut.us/websters/iipguide.htm>

"At the bottom of the web page, there must be an indication of the date of the last update to that page and the name or initials of the person(s) responsible for the page or update. It shall be that person's responsibility to keep the web page current."

Lakeville Area Public Schools, *District Web Policy* <http://www.isd194.k12.mn.us/webpoly.htm>

"At the bottom of the page, there must a link that returns the user to the appropriate points in the district pages. This would normally be a return to the district home page."

Minneapolis Public Schools District #1, *World Wide Web Page Development Guidelines* <http://www.mpls.k12.mn.us/policies/6415D.html>

"Only scripts that are deemed to be secure and widely acceptable to users will be installed. The Internet Administrator retains the right to limit any scripts that use excessive bandwidth or compromise network security."

Calgary Board of Education, *Acceptable Posting Practice* <http://www.cbe.ab.ca/intranet2/app.htm>

Some documents created by the school or district are considered public and can be accessed by any visitor to the Web site. Other documents might be published only on a school or district Intranet, or might not be released at all. It is important for school and district Web authors to know which materials belong in which areas so that nothing inadvertently becomes available to the public that is intended for internal use only.

The following types of materials are commonly recommended for school Web sites:

1 Information about the school

2 Principal's message

3 Parent handbooks

4 Student projects

5 E-libraries

The following types of materials are commonly kept on school Intranets or are not published at all:

1. Staff directories
2. Student directories
3. Photographs of students or classes
4. Union agreements or other internal documents

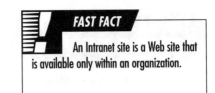

All pages should be checked for spelling and grammar before being published on the Web. Although this is an expectation on any Web site, it is even more important for schools. Schools or districts may decide to publish the best examples of student work or all student work. If students are producing opinion pieces as assignments or for school newsletters, these pieces should be vetted to ensure high quality.

In *Beginner's Handbook: Developing Web Pages for School and Classroom* (Teacher Created Materials, Inc., 1998), Susan Hixson and Kathleen Schrock point out, "All [student] work should be edited before being posted. After all, this work is a reflection on the school as well as [on] the student and teacher." Schools should examine student work not only for style and structure but also for appropriate content. *Implementing and Managing Web Site Development in Education* <http://www.learning.gov.ab.ca/ technology/ bestpractices/pdf/websitedevelopment.pdf> notes, "The courts have ruled that schools have the right to limit freedom of expression in publications in cases where that expression might conflict with community values." *Legal and Ethical Issues Related to the Use of the Internet in K–12 Schools* <http://206.98.102.208/documents/ leicontent.html>, a publication of the Center for Advanced Technologies in Education (CATE), gives an overview of some Supreme Court cases surrounding student speech on the Internet. According to CATE, the following content restrictions appear to be appropriate for school districts to impose:

1. Criminal speech and speech in the course of committing a crime
2. Speech that is inappropriate in an educational setting or violates district rules necessary to maintain a quality educational environment (inappropriate language, dangerous information, violations of privacy, abuse of resources, copyright infringement or plagiarism, violations of personal safety)
3. Educationally-relevant restrictions (quality of writing, adequacy of research, appropriateness to school activities)

IDEAS IN ACTION

ARCHIVING THE SCHOOL WEB SITE

Arbor Heights Elementary School in Seattle, Washington, has maintained an impressive archive of its site online at <**http://www.halcyon.com/arborhts/history.html**>. The archive contains brief notes about the Arbor Heights Elementary School Web site since it began in 1994 and contains actual pages used over the years. The history section contains pages from 1994 through 1996, with the archives for "1997 to the present" listed at the bottom of the "What's New" page. The collection is an amazing testament to the evolution of school sites since the early days of the Web and to the commitment by the educators who have worked hard to maintain them.

Figure 4.1 Arbor Heights Elementary School Archives

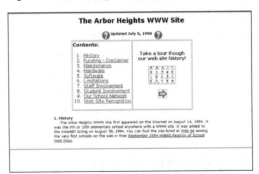

<**http://www.halcyon.com/arborhts/ahfaq.html**> Arbor Heights Elementary School has archived its site since 1994, forming an impressive historical example of how the site has evolved. *Mark Ahlness, Arbor Heights Elementary School, Seattle, Washington*

"School-sponsored organizations, including school clubs, school and home clubs, and school and parent groups may have homepages. Content of these pages must be approved by the school principal. It is the responsibility of the organization to update and maintain the information. The homepage of any school sponsored organization must reside on the district server."

Cupertino Union School District, *World Wide Web Guidelines*
<http://www.cupertino.k12.ca.us/Do.www/W3guide.html>

"Many departments work with sensitive materials that involve privacy issues, school data, and/or potential political issues. It is very important that the Director of Communications is consulted prior to publication of these kinds of materials to insure that the information is presented in a complete and accurate context."

Hillsboro School District Web Publishing Guidelines
<http://www.hsd.k12.or.us/district/technology/webpublish.htm>

"All work must be free of any spelling or grammatical errors. Documents may not contain objectionable material or point directly to objectionable material."

Mankato School District 77, *World Wide Web Page Creation Guidelines*
<http://www.isd77.k12.mn.us/webguide.html>

"Pages may not contain links to other pages that are not yet completed."

Grand Erie District School Board, *Web Publishing Guidelines*
<http://www.whs.on.ca/webpublishingdoc.doc>

"Web pages will be deleted when a student graduates or moves unless prior arrangements have been made with the media specialist or network specialist."

Winona School District 861, *Creating and Placing Web Pages*
<http://www.luminet.net/wmstechnology/861.WebPagesPolicy.html>

Once pages are published, how often should they be maintained and how long should they stay on the server? Just as other documents produced within an organization have retention periods, Web pages can also have a life span. Madison Metropolitan School District <http://www.madison.k12.wi.us/hpguides.htm> provides its schools with a general maintenance schedule that lists items that need to be updated at the beginning of the year and those that need to be updated throughout the year. Content guidelines and policies can outline how long certain materials should be available on the site and what happens to them when the time limit is reached. Publishing guidelines can give direction on which materials will be moved to an electronic archive, sent to the records management department of the district, or eliminated. It is important to be in contact with the records management group in the district for direction surrounding some of these retention periods, as some legal requirements may need to be addressed.

► COMMERCIAL CONTENT

Now more than ever, schools need to examine the issue of commercial content on their Web sites. Commercial content can be advertising, linking, shopping, and fund raising. Schools often have partnerships with commercial organizations, and these partnerships can be recognized by linking to partner Web sites. Sometimes advertising banners or logos must be displayed in exchange for the use of free scripts or services from third parties. Some of the free hosting services designed for schools are doing a subtle, but powerful, form of marketing to students, parents, and the schools. Guidelines that outline what kind of commercial links are permitted will help schools ensure that links are an educational benefit rather than simply free advertising.

Some school districts have policies that do not allow any kind of commercial aspect on school Web sites. However, they may need to revisit policies in light of newer developments on the Web: The commerce ability of the Web can be turned into fund-raising opportunities for the school.

▷ SAFETY AND LIABILITY GUIDELINES

Safety and liability issues for school Web sites are bound to be the most controversial aspect while creating and reviewing school Web publishing guidelines and policies. What may seem an obvious policy to one person is not necessarily so to another, and restrictions and revisions are sure to meet with stiff resistance from some individuals. In her article, "What Are Your Students Publishing on the Web?" (*The School Administrator Web Edition*, April 1998, available at <http:// www.aasa.org/publications/ sa/1998_04/ Perkins-Bowen.htm>), Candace Perkins Bowen refers to the work of Jonathan Wallace, computer law expert and author of *Sex, Laws and Cyberspace*. Perkins notes that "new media often face strict laws and regulations at first, which over time become more relaxed as the public begins to understand the latest means of communication. In other instances, case law becomes a costly but definitive way to resolve the challenges." The question becomes, what school wants to be the test case?

FAST FACT

"The critical legal question in the event of problems arising from the use of the Internet will be whether the district had exercised reasonable precautions against a foreseeable risk."

—*Legal and Ethical Issues Related to the Use of the Internet in K–12 Schools*
<http://206.98.102.208/documents/leicontent.html>

QUICK TIP

TRY IT YOURSELF!

1 Select the name of one of your students or staff

2 Select an online directory

3 Type in the last name, along with the city and state of your school

4 Consider whether the results could be narrowed down using information from your school Web site (location of the school, parents' names, links to personal sites)

5 If you find a likely home address, go to a map creation tool such as www.mapquest.com

6 Type in the address you located to have a map drawn

The more information someone has, the easier it becomes to locate the student or staff member using these tools on the Internet.

The most common issues in school Web publishing guidelines and policies surround personal privacy and how much information schools can or should publish on their Web sites. Posting personal information, staff or student photos, and e-mail addresses is controversial. Publishing student work brings forth another set of issues, including concerns about copyright and content liability. In addition, how are materials handled that are created by those who are not students? Educators are excited about the capabilities of Web publishing, but balancing enthusiasm and common sense is essential. Just what are some of the issues, how serious are they, and what guidelines and policies are schools using to manage them?

Personal Information

Most educators are quick to agree that schools should not release too much personal information, but exactly how much is too much? Jack Dale, an educator and technology leader with the Calgary Board of Education in Calgary, Alberta, says that schools need to really assess whether the information they want to give out is "need to know" or "nice to know." Because schools are dealing with an electronic, global environment that is easily searchable using automated tools, cautions apply that simply are not the same as when producing print material for students to take home. Schools do not always know what is happening in the lives of staff and students beyond the doors of the school and should show respect for privacy. Although giving out information may be legal, sometimes it may not be in the best interests of the staff or students involved.

Some schools publish staff e-mail addresses so parents can easily contact teachers with concerns or for information. Dale's comment: "Is there a safer way the school can provide that information to local parents?" He points out that automated tools on the Web regularly harvest e-mail addresses from Web pages and sell them to bulk mailing companies, which increases the volume of junk mail coming into teachers' mail accounts. Will staff members with privacy concerns be conspicuous by their absence from the e-mail listing on the Web page? Will a missing staff e-mail imply to parents that some teachers are not interested in communicating?

In the case of student information, Dale notes, "If you can narrow a student down to a school and find a picture, you have a good opportunity for abduction." With students producing Web sites inside and outside of the school environment (often linking the two), it has become increasingly easy to find exactly this type of information. Information such as unique or full names, the location of the school, grade levels of students, and personal information and interests—all combine with online phone directories, reverse directories, and online map builders to make it easy to collect disparate information into a reasonable sketch of a student. Abductors generally spend time profiling their target, and schools must consider how much they aid the process.

In July 2000, *eSchool News* contained an article pointing out the risks of publishing student information on school sites, and voiced the concerns and recommendations of FBI officers who work in this field. "Pedophiles using the Internet often initiate contact with their victims through online chat rooms, according to the FBI, and they later visit school web sites looking for more information about the children they've encountered. Pedophiles who find pictures and information on school web pages can then show up at the school looking for specific children . . ." (Branigan, Cara. "FBI Urges Schools to Ban Web-site Student Photos, but Not All Educators Agree." *eSchool News,* July 24, 2000 <http://www.eschoolnews.com/showstory.cfm?ArticleID=1342>).

In light of these concerns, most schools have fairly strict guidelines and policies surrounding the publishing of personal information and photographs on the school Web site. Schools that do post personal information should have standard forms requiring parental

"Never identify photographs of students by name; make certain that no one can clearly associate a name and a face in single and group photographs."

Germantown Academy, *GAnet Acceptable Publication Policy*
<http://www.gemantownacademy.com/Oursite/APP.html>

"Web documents shall not include a student's home phone number, address or the names of other family members or friends."

"Neither students, staff, nor other individuals may use the district's web pages to provide access to their personal pages on other servers or online services."

Grande Erie District School Board, *Web Publishing Guidelines*
<http://www.whs.on.ca/webpublishingdoc.doc>

"No student email addresses for any student who publishes a page should be listed on the student's Web page."

Hillsboro School District, *Web Publishing Guidelines*
<http://www.hsd.k12.or.us/district/technology/webpublish.htm>

"No pictures of students (video or still) or audio clips will be published without written and dated permission from the student's parent or guardian."

Minneapolis Public Schools District #1, *World Wide Web Page Development Guidelines* <http://www.mpls.k12.mn.us/policies/6415D.html>

permission that must be completed and kept on file. The most common policies in this area include the following:

1. No full names of students (initials, first names, or combinations only)
2. No full names of staff without written permission from the staff member
3. No personal information, such as home addresses or phone numbers
4. No staff photographs without written permission from the staff member
5. No student photographs without written permission from parents or guardians
6. No photographs of individual students (groups only)
7. No photographs in which students can be identified individually
8. Pictures showing groups at a distance only
9. Photographs facing at an angle
10. No faces that are identifiable
11. No names associated with student photographs
12. No individual student e-mail addresses (group addresses only)
13. No links to personal pages from school pages

The preceding examples are common in most school Web publishing guidelines and policies. Yet some people feel that taking this stance is unnecessary and overly restrictive. In "What Are Your Students Publishing on the Web," Candace Perkins Bowen states, "School leaders have no basis for concern that the publishing of names and faces is a legal risk." Global Schoolhouse notes in its series of articles on "Building a Collaborative Web Project" <http://gsh.lightspan.com/web/webproj/define/protect/pubnames.htm>, that while there are many debates, "There is no clear consensus on this question, nor are there any legal guidelines." What that means is that the decision remains with the school or district as to how much personal information is too much, and it is yet to be fully tested in the courts.

Publishing the Work of Students

School Web sites are a perfect place to highlight student work and to provide students with a real-life learning environment. Students create knowledge and get feedback from the global audience instead of from teachers or peers only. Adding student work to school and district Web sites requires thoughtful consideration of guidelines and policies that are needed to address copyright issues. Schools and districts may need legal counsel in creating policies and permission forms for these issues. The primary point to address deals with ownership—whoever owns the work must get acknowledgment for it. This includes materials gathered from the Web or other sources, works created by students, and items created by staff or volunteers.

The easiest way to ensure compliance with copyright laws is to provide Web authors with direction on what requires permission and how to get permission. Producing form letters and permission forms for specific items and making those available through the Web site facilitates compliance by school and district Web authors with the guidelines and policies. Items related to copyright that appear in school and district Web publishing policies should include obtaining *written* permission to do the following:

1. Use copyrighted works
2. Publish student work
3. Publish the work of volunteers

Those creating Web pages commonly want to use graphics and text from other Web sites. Start incorporating lessons about computer ethics with students as early as possible in their learning. Students must understand that publishing the work of others without written permission is illegal. Suggest that students request permission from site owners to use copyrighted works. Tell

---

 RESOURCE BOX

PERMISSION FORMS

Spring Branch Independent School District
<http://www.spring-branch.isd.tenet.edu/admin/tcom/policy/exhibit_a.htm>
This is a sample form for permission, covering student name, photograph, video or audio recording, and student work.

Richmond, British Columbia
<http://www.sd38.bc.ca/WebPolicy/Web_Policy/RSB_Web_Pages16.html>
Richmond has a release form for student personal information that includes name, photograph, or e-mail address.

West Loogootee Elementary School
<http://www.siec.k12.in.us/~west/article/permission.htm>
This sample form for student and guardian provides permission for student first name, photograph, or project.

SAMPLE PERMISSION FORM

WEB PUBLISHING PERMISSION FORM

Date: _____

Name of Student: _____

Project Name: _____

    Signing this form gives permission for your child's work to be published on the (Name of School) Web site on the Internet. Your son's or daughter's work will be published with a copyright notice prohibiting further copying of that work without express written permission. If permission to reprint is requested, the request will be forwarded to you.

    For safety reasons, your son's or daughter's name will not appear on the Web site. The address of the Web page will be sent home with your son or daughter.

I grant permission that my son's/daughter's work may be published on the World Wide Web as detailed in the above description.

Parent/Guardian Signature _____ **Date**_____

I, the student, give my permission for the described publication of my work.

Student Signature _____ **Date**_____

students that works do not have to have a copyright notice to be protected by copyright. Even the youngest students can request permission to use someone else's work if the teacher provides a simple form letter.

    Schools must have signed permission forms from students and their parents/guardians before publishing student work on the school Web site. (A sample of a standard permission form for publishing student work follows this section.) Using a permission form demonstrates an acknowledgment of the students' creativity and hard work and makes it clear that they do legally "own" the work. Students whose works are protected will find it easier to understand why they must get permission to use the work of someone else. **Because students are owners of their work, schools and districts are infringing on copyright if they publish student work without permission.** Standard permission forms are legal documents that demonstrate compliance by the school or district with current copyright law.

Publishing Work Created by Volunteers or Staff Members

Similar rights exist for work created for the school by volunteers and, in some cases, by staff members. However, these situations are rarely treated in school and district publishing guidelines and policies at this time. If volunteers have contributed photographs or digitized images or have created graphics or written work, these items are protected by copyright and are the property of the individuals who have created the works. School and district publishing guidelines and policies should include direction for handling these works as well. Where did the individuals get the material? If they gathered it from elsewhere, the same copyright permissions are required as when students are using the work of others. If volunteers have personally created the material, they must release it to the school for use. Again, a standard permission form can be extremely helpful in taking care of these necessary details.

What about works created by staff members? "Copyright Office Circular 1: Copyright Basics: Who Can Claim Copyright" (*United States Copyright Office,* December 2000) <http://www.loc.gov/copyright/circs/circ1.html#wccc> states that the employer owns the work if it is "prepared by an employee within the scope of his or her employment." Works created within the scope of employment are called "works for hire." Only under special conditions does ownership belong to the creator of works for hire. Works created outside of the scope of employment (i.e., done at home on the employees' own time, with their own equipment, and not actually assigned as part of their job) *could* belong to the creator rather than to the school or district. Schools in these situations may need to have the authors release these works to the school or district through a permission form, just as in the case of a volunteer. Noting when these permission forms are required, and how and where to get them, is an important part of the school or district publishing guidelines and policies.

SAMPLES OF *PUBLISHING STUDENT OR EXTERNAL WORK* GUIDELINES FROM SCHOOL AND DISTRICT POLICIES

"Publications must include a statement of copyright when appropriate and indicate that permission has been secured when including copyrighted materials."

Hillsboro School District, *Web Publishing Guidelines*
<http://www.hsd.k12.or.us/district/technology/webpublish.htm>

"No original student work will be published without written and dated permission from the student's parent or guardian."

Minneapolis Public Schools District #1, *World Wide Web Page Development Guidelines*
<http://www.mpls.k12.mn.us/policies/6415D.html>

"For each re-publishing (on a Web site or file server) of a graphic or a text file which was produced externally, there must be a notice at the bottom of the page crediting the original producer and noting how and when permission was granted."
"Students and staff engaged in producing Web pages must provide library media specialists with e-mail or hard copy permissions to file before the Web pages are actually published. . . . In the case of 'public domain' documents, printed evidence must be provided to document the status of the materials."

Bellingham Public Schools, *Web Publishing Rules*
<http://www.bham.wednet.edu/copyrule.htm>

"All work to be submitted for publication must be the original work of the student. . . . all sources used within must be fully acknowledged and a complete bibliography to be published with the work."

Cerdon College, *Publication of Student Work on the Internet*
<http://www.schools.ash.org.au/cerdon/policies/interpol.htm>

Are schools and districts liable for what is published on their Web sites? That depends on a number of factors and which legal acts apply. The Center for Advanced Technologies in Education (CATE) tries to provide some clarification in the document *Legal and Ethical Issues Related to the Use of the Internet in K–12 Schools* <http://206.98.102.208/documents/leicontent.html>. "The Computer Decency Act provides immunity for 'interactive service providers' for material that is transmitted through their system, but not for 'information content providers.'. . . If the district establishes a district web site, the district is also an information content provider and can be held liable to publisher standards for any defamatory material posted on the site." Schools and districts are viewed as "interactive service providers" when they offer Internet access. They are "information content providers" when they publish Web sites. The Online Copyright Infringement Liability Limitation Act provides interactive service providers with an exemption from monetary damages for copyright infringement, but only if the provider is not directly involved with the placement of the material. Therefore, schools and districts that upload all pages centrally instead of having individuals within the schools uploading could come into difficulty depending on the case in question. (Detailed information surrounding copyright issues is covered in Chapter 5, *Copyright Issues and the Web*.)

▶ RESPONSIBILITY GUIDELINES

Chapter 6, *Gathering Resources . . . Just Who Is Needed?,* suggests who should be part of school and district Web teams and what their responsibilities might include. Though not all of these people need to be listed in publishing guidelines, some key contacts are necessary. Bellingham Public Schools gives an overview to the roles various people play in the development of their school Web sites <http://www.bham.wednet.edu/homepage.htm>. Minneapolis Public Schools District #1 <http://www.mpls.k12.mn.us/policies/6415D.html> has a section of its guidelines with clear statements of responsibility surrounding uploads, who can author, web site functionality, and who deals with content issues. This type of information will help staff, students, parents, and Web authors pinpoint the right person in the shortest possible time in the event of a question or problem.

Guidelines surrounding responsibility should also include who is responsible for proofreading materials for quality of writing and content, for gathering and maintaining "Web files" that contain permission and release forms, and for uploading the pages on the Internet. If external groups are represented on the school Web site, the guidelines must clarify who is permitted to develop this content—will content development be limited to students and staff, or can external organizations create their own?

▶ KEEPING THE GUIDELINES AND POLICIES CURRENT

Technology is constantly changing, which means guidelines and policies that govern the use of technology must change as well. A school or district must regularly revisit its set of publishing guidelines and polices to ensure that they are still applicable. Without definite plans for revision, the Web publishing guidelines will become static, quickly go out of date, and leave school and district staff stranded as the Web evolves. At the end of the Winona School District guidelines, a statement addressing revisions assigns the task and creates an open-ended schedule along with the requirement for an annual revision. "Given the rapid change in technology, some of the technical standards outlined in this policy may require change throughout the year. Such changes will be made by the District network specialist with approval of the Superintendent. This Web Page Policy will be updated on an annual basis, or more frequently if required" <http://wms.luminet.net/wmstechnology/ 861.WebPagesPolicy.html>. By stating this requirement in their Web publishing guidelines and policies, schools and districts are building living documents that are bound to change with technology.

"Teachers are responsible for the content of all class based Web pages."

Richmond School Board, *Web Site Content Restrictions and Responsibilities*
<http://www.sd38.bc.ca/WebPolicy/Web_Policy/RSB_Web_Pages05.html>

"Final decisions regarding access to active Web pages for editing content or organization will rest with the building principal, with input from the media specialist and/or the network specialist."

Winona School District 861, *Creating and Placing Web Pages*
<http://www.luminet.net/wmstechnology/861.WebPagesPolicy.html>

"At least two people should be designated to access the servers, maintain the information in a timely manner, and check websites for broken links."

Cupertino Union School District, *World Wide Web Guidelines*
<http://www.cupertino.k12.ca.us/Do.www/W3guide.html>

"The webmaster will make himself available to receive submissions from teachers, staff, and students of Sacred Heart School, to review the material to verify it meets the editorial guidelines. Then he will update the web site to include the new material in a timely manner. . . . The webmaster will make periodic backups of the web site so if damage (inadvertent or deliberate) does occur, the web site can be restored from a recent backup."

Sacred Heart School Web Site Policy
<http://www.mcraeclan.com/SHS/SHSWebPolicy.htm>

"Directory structure will be determined by the local Site Administrator and/or Manager of Information Technology and the building person(s) responsible for coordinating the school's web pages."

Grande Erie District School Board, *Web Publishing Guidelines*
<http://www.whs.on.ca/webpublishingdoc.doc>

"The principal of the school will name a 'webmaster' who will serve as the editor of the web site. The webmaster will be responsible for receiving submissions, updating the web site, and adhering to all the guidelines listed here. . . . The webmaster will document the procedures used to administer the web site so that another person would be able to step in if the webmaster is unavailable."

Sacred Heart School Web Site Policy
<http://www.mcraeclan.com/SHS/SHSWebPolicy.htm>

"[Web pages] must be approved for content, spelling, & grammar by the campus principal, administrative department head or their designee. Principals and department heads are responsible for accuracy and appropriateness of information at the campus/department level. . . . [Web pages are] then given to the District Web Specialist for publication. The web specialist will also proof both copy and code to be sure the pages are in keeping with district practices in regard to content, links, copyright adorns and code viability."

Spring Branch Independent School District, *SBISD Electronic Communication and Data Management Guidelines*
<http://www.spring-branch.isd.tenet.edu/admin/tcom/policy/guidelines.htm>

"The school Webmaster acts as the school's liaison with Instructional Technology staff training and information regarding the issues of online publishing and web use."

Hillsboro School District, *Web Publishing Guidelines*
<http://www.hsd.k12.or.us/district/technology/webpublish.htm>

"Where links are provided to non-District created/controlled sites, appropriate disclaimers shall be provided next to the link. . . . The home page of a District, school or school-sponsored activity site having sponsors shall have a link labeled "Sponsors." That link shall open a page listing the sponsors. The page will contain a disclaimer that may express appreciation for the support of all sponsors, but shall also state that listing of the sponsor(s) should not be construed as implying Board, school, or activity endorsement or promotion of any sponsor's products and/or services."

Madison City Schools, *School Systems and School Web Sites*
<http://www.madisoncity.k12.al.us/Policies/IFBGA.htm>

"Each page sponsored on DSD sponsored sites shall contain a disclaimer stating that published content adheres to these guidelines. The disclaimer should contain a link to the online version of the guidelines . . ."

Davis School District Internet/Intranet Publishing Guidelines
<http://www.davis.k12.ut.us/websters/iipguide.htm>

RESOURCE BOX

SAMPLES OF DISCLAIMER STATEMENTS OR POLICIES

Mount Carmel Area School District
Legal Notices and Trademarks
<http://www.mca.k12.pa.us/legal.html>

Valley Elementary School
Valley Elementary School Legal Notice
<http://pc38.ve.weber.k12.ut.us/LegalNotice/VESCopyright.html>

Both Mount Carmel Area School District and Valley Elementary School have disclaimer information on their Web sites.

▷ ADDING DISCLAIMERS

It is a good practice to add disclaimers to school Web sites and pages. While the disclaimer does not release the school from following responsible publishing practices, it does demonstrate that the school is trying to exercise diligence in its Web publishing.

Disclaimers can point visitors to policies on intellectual freedom and publishing standards that the school or district is trying to maintain. This can help in the event of challenges to the content on the site. Disclaimers should also warn visitors that links to Web sites on the Internet are beyond the control of the school, and that hyperlinks and content on those sites may disappear, move, or change without notice.

Schools and districts can make a disclaimer a requirement by stating the disclaimer in the publishing guidelines and policies. Some schools and districts require short, general disclaimers that appear on each Web page (often in a footer) or specific types of Web pages on the site. Other schools and districts have longer disclaimers or policies that Web authors are expected to link to from each page.

➤ THE RULES OF THE ROAD . . . PROTECTING OR RESTRICTING?

The development of publishing guidelines and policies is usually done at the district level, sometimes with little input from the schools, and they are handed down with the rest of the rules and regulations for the district. (**See** *Publishing Guidelines and Policies Check Sheet* in **Appendix 1.**) Because of this, some educators view publishing guidelines and policies as restrictions created by those who do not work in classrooms and hence do not understand what classroom teachers really need. However, what classroom teachers really need is a safe environment to work in and sound educational reasons for creating Web pages. By focusing on creating valuable spaces for learning within the parameters of the school or district publishing guidelines and policies and not dwelling on what they are not permitted to do, good educators create amazing Web pages.

Publishing guidelines and policies are often viewed as the bone-dry, boring part of creating school Web sites. However, as the "rules of the road," school and district publishing guidelines serve to keep everyone from getting lost, getting hit, or getting hurt through the Web. They are in place to make sure the Internet continues to be a valuable and useful resource for everyone in the school or district. They provide boundaries so students have opportunities to learn real-life skills in a live environment—one where they must think before they publish.

Chapter 5

Copyright Issues and the Web

'Twas brillig, and the slithy toves
Did gyre and gimble in the wabe;
All mimsy were the borogoves,
and the mome raths outgrabe.

—Lewis Carroll

D oes reading or hearing about copyright invoke thoughts of Lewis Carroll's *Jabberwocky* from his *Through the Looking Glass* (1872)? This chapter is intended to help the reader better understand copyright basics as they relate to the Internet and Web sites. While this brief overview of United States Copyright Law and Guidelines and *the Copyright Check Sheet* in **Appendix 1** are based on extensive research, they are not intended to take the place of legal counsel. Consult with an attorney who is knowledgeable about copyright for answers to legal questions and for additional legal advice and guidance.

▷ WHAT? IT ISN'T ALL "FREE"?

A prevailing assumption is that everything found on the Web is free and in the public domain. In fact, quite the opposite is true. Almost everything on the Internet is protected by copyright. Since 1989, even works without a copyright notice and ones that give anybody permission to copy them are usually protected by copyright. In 1989, the United States signed an international copyright treaty that is known as the Berne Convention. Most countries are members of this convention. By signing the treaty, the participating nations agreed to abide by one another's copyright laws.

When the United States became a member of the Berne Convention, U. S. copyright laws were adjusted to better align with those of the other member nations. As a result, copyright registration of a work is no longer a requirement for a work to be protected by copyright. A work does not even need to have a copyright notice to be protected. **As soon as a work is in a tangible form, it is copyrighted. That means that as soon as a Web page is saved to a disk or a hard drive, it is protected by copyright.** Unless the content of a Web page is old enough to be in the public domain or is created by a U.S. government official in the course of duty, the content is protected by copyright.

The word *copyright* means the right to copy. The Copyright Act gives the copyright holder six rights:

1 **REPRODUCTION** is the right to copy or reproduce. (**Digital Notes:** Making a digital copy for the Web or for a download is a form of reproduction. Printing a Web page is also a form of reproduction.)

2 **ADAPTATION** is the right to prepare derivatives or adaptations of the work. (**Digital Notes:** Changing the format of an item is a form of adaptation, as is changing a resource from a print to a Web version. Altering an item, and copying someone's HTML and changing it to your content are adaptations. HTML stands for Hypertext Markup Language-see Glossary.)

3 **DISTRIBUTION** is the right to distribute copies of the work to the public. (**Digital Notes:** Placing a copy on the Web or making another electronic transmission of a work is a form of distribution.)

4 **PUBLIC PERFORMANCE** is the right to perform work in public. This includes broadcasts, digital transmissions, and live renditions of those works. (**Digital Notes:** Digital transmissions are public performances.)

5 **PUBLIC DISPLAY** is the right to publicly display (including digital version) a musical, dramatic, literary, pictorial, graphic, pantomime, sculptural, or choreographic work. (**Digital Notes:** Digital transmissions are public displays.)

6 **DIGITAL AUDIO TRANSMISSIONS OF SOUND RECORDINGS** is the right to digitally transmit audio sound recordings. (**Digital Notes:** Sending or downloading a musical or other audio recording over the Internet is a digital transmission.)

Others must ask permission of the copyright holder to reproduce, adapt, distribute, publicly perform, publicly display, or digitally transmit audio sound recordings, unless the intended use falls within a category called **fair use**.

WHEN IS EDUCATIONAL USE FAIR?

Under section 107 of the Copyright Act, educators are conditionally permitted to use copyrighted materials. There are four factors used to determine fair use:

1 What is the **purpose** and **character** of the use? Is the work for nonprofit educational use or for commercial use?

2 What is the **nature** of the original work? The use of a creative or fictional work is less likely to be found to be fair use than the use of a factual work. The use of published works is more likely to be found fair than the use of unpublished works.

3 What is the **amount** and **substantiality** of the portion of the work being used relative to the complete original work?

4 Will the use **affect** the **potential market** or value of the original work? Only the *likelihood* of harm has to be proven to be a violation.

Consider all four factors in determining fair use. If a suit is brought against an educator, the educator is in the position of having to prove fair use. When defendants claim fair use, they are admitting to the infringement. Ultimately, the courts will make a decision if use is fair.

Congressional committees have created guidelines to help educators understand and honor fair use. These guidelines should be used in addition to the preceding guidelines for further clarification.

Use the three **classroom fair use test questions** to help make decisions about fair use:

1 **Spontaneity:** Is the educational use made at the last moment when there is not enough time to contact the copyright holder? This is a fuzzy question when dealing with the Web. E-mail can be a nearly instantaneous form of communication, but it can also be a futile process. Not everyone reads his or her e-mail regularly, and some people do not answer e-mail. The copyright holder is not required to respond to requests.

2 **Brevity:** What is the amount being used relative to the whole work? If the portion being used is the "heart" of a piece, it may not be used even if it is a small amount of the original.

3 **Cumulative Effect:** Will the use impact the item's market or value? Market and value can be impacted even if money is not involved.

WHAT DOES THIS MEAN FOR EDUCATIONAL WEB SITES?

Copying other people's materials to Web sites without written permission is a violation of copyright laws unless the materials are in the public domain. Putting copied materials on a Web site infringes on the author's rights of reproduction, distribution, public performance, and public display. Changing the format of a work to place it on the Web violates the copyright holder's rights of adaptation and distribution. Including sound recordings on Web sites violates the author's right to digital audio transmissions of sound recordings.

Posting copied materials to the Web is extremely unlikely to fall under fair use. Even if the purpose of a Web site is educational, accessing it is not confined to a classroom unless the site is password protected. Putting materials on Web sites could easily impact potential market and

OBTAINING WRITTEN PERMISSION

When writing to secure written permission to use a copyrighted work, address the request to the copyright holder or to the Permissions Department of a commercial entity. Requests to use copyrighted materials can be e-mailed. There are 10 components to be included in a basic request form:

1 Identify the work to be reprinted by including the title, author/editor, edition, and date. For Web materials, also include the URL.

2 Describe the exact portions (pages, images, footage, other) of the work to be used. Include a copy of that portion.

3 Explain how the work is to be used and the purpose of the use. Indicate if use is educational.

4 Give the address of the Web site on which the work will appear.

5 Indicate the number of copies to be made. (This type of information is traditionally included on a form for permission to use copyrighted materials. It may not be applicable for requesting to use materials on the Web.) For Web use, indicate if the materials will be publicly accessible or password protected.

6 Include the duration of the use of the copy. How long will it be posted on the Internet?

7 Tell the nature of copies to be made. Will the item be scanned, photocopied, or reproduced by another method?

8 Explain how the copies are to be distributed (e.g., classroom Web page, newsletter, closed circuit TV, and so forth).

9 Ask how the copyright holder is to be credited.

10 List the name and contact information (address, phone number, fax number, and so forth) of the person making the request.

BE PREPARED:

1 Do not be surprised if a fee is required for use of the material or if the owner declines.

2 **If you decide not to use the materials after obtaining permission, notify the rights broker that you will not be using them. Otherwise, if there is a fee, the copyright holder will expect to be paid.**

3 Keep a copy of the completed permission form and any receipts on file.

4 Follow any restrictions or conditions of use.

value. A good rule is "When in doubt, don't." Do, however, ask permission to use others' work on the Web. The answer may be yes. If a work is already on the Web, link to it, do not copy it, and tell the webmaster you have done so. Webmasters are less likely to move or remove pages that they know are useful to others.

Copyright law also has implications for publishing or showcasing student works on the Web. **Student-created work** is protected by copyright and should not be published on the Web without express written permission from both the student and the student's parent or guardian. Obtain permission for each work to be posted on the Internet. All school districts should have guidelines and a permission form for publishing student works on the Internet. (**See Chapter 4**, *Blueprints for a Firm Foundation: Publishing Guidelines and Policies,* for information about creating Web publishing policies/guidelines.) When publishing student work on the Web, follow district Web publishing policies/guidelines regarding using students' names on the Web.

Some materials come with permission statements or licenses that spell out acceptable use. If **graphics** or **animations** are found on a clip art Web site, search for some kind of statement that tells how the images may be used. These statements may indicate that there has to be an advertising image that links to the original Web site. If that is an acceptable condition, use the graphic. Before using any graphics found on the Internet, use common sense. Some sites have posted pirated graphics. Look for clues that posted graphics are or are not pirated. Keep a record of any images used. **See** the *Image Source Note Sheet* in **Appendix 1**.

Some school districts have a Web publishing policy or guideline against having any kind of commercial content on Web sites. In those districts, Web workers are not able to use that kind of clip art. Even purchased copies of clip art may have use restrictions. The license may or may not permit the use of the clip art on the Web. If Web publishing is permitted, specific wording may have to accompany the art. It may be required to credit the work on each page or include an advertising image with a link to the copyright holder's Web site. Again, check the district's Web publishing policies/guidelines before using advertising images on a Web site. Credit whatever clip art is used. On an "About This Web Site" page, list with simple links the source(s) of all clip art used on a Web site.

Be particularly cautious before putting **music** and **motion media** on a Web site. A high percentage of these materials that are on the Internet are in violation of copyright laws. It is possible to purchase "royalty-free" music, photos, and so forth. Check these collections for the same types of restrictions that accompany the use of clip art.

What can be safely put on a Web site? The safest items to include in a Web site are original materials. Ideas, concepts, processes, systems, operation methods, procedures, facts, principles, and discoveries are *not* protected by copyright, but wording *is* protected. If using these types of factual materials, avoid creating what is in fact an adaptation/derivation. Therefore, it is wise to obtain information from multiple sources and to do more than simply rearrange or make minor modifications.

FAST FACT

The ownership of Web sites can be a gray area. Educational Web sites may or may not "belong" to school systems.

Web sites created "within the scope of employment" are "works made for hire" and are likely to be the property of a school system.

When school Web sites are created on an employee's own time, of the employee's own volition, on personal equipment, and housed on an independent Web server, the employee has a strong case for owning the Web site. Because Web sites may be created under most, but not all, of these conditions, ownership may not be clear-cut.

When volunteers create Web pages, ownership can be questionable.

Note: Some teacher contracts may specify ownership of school-related work.

QUICK TIP

Keep careful records of the sources of all clip art. Use the Source of Image Note Sheet (see **Appendix 1**) for recording where the images are found and the corresponding usage restrictions and guidelines. Place copies of information about usage restrictions and copies of licenses in a file folder labeled "Image Use." Clearly label which clip art images are covered by the various licenses and guidelines.

QUICK TIP

Visit Joyce Valenza's Web page, *Public Domain Images for Use in Multimedia Projects and Web Pages* < http://mciu.org/ ~spjvweb/cfimages.html> for links to images that may be used in educational projects. Check each site for information regarding use.

FAST FACT

Photographers are the copyright holders of the pictures that they take. When putting photos on the Web, obtain permission from both the photographer and the person(s) in the photograph. If the person pictured is a minor, the parent's/guardian's consent is required.

▶ GRAY AREAS

Links

Linking is a great alternative to copying. **Links** are facts, such as phone numbers, and cannot be copyrighted. Think of them as cross-references. Be aware of some cautions when creating links:

1 Do not copy lists of links or their annotations. Although Web URLs are not protected by copyright, a list of links is a compiled work and, as such, is protected by copyright. It is acceptable to use a few links from another site with additional links that the Web creator has found and collected. In its *How to Create Menus That Deliver* Web page <http://www.bham.wednet.edu/howto.htm>, Bellingham Schools warns to eliminate 50% or more of a list's links and to add additional links before using links from another list. If links are used from other sources, credit the original sources.

2 Give the user the option of removing the frame if a site is constructed with frames. The framing site must make it clear to the user that the "link-to site" content belongs to another site.

3 Do not deep link if other webmasters have requested no deep linking. That means that the webmasters prefer that links be made to their home page instead of to a page that is buried deep in the site. This may be because of advertising that helps to pay for the site or because of use counters. (Counters record the number of times a page has been visited.) When Web pages with advertisements and counters are bypassed, a site's funding may be jeopardized. Ultimately, the Web site may be removed from the Web due to loss of funding. Some copyright experts state that this is not a copyright issue; however, others indicate that copyright problems with deep linking could arise in the future.

4 Obtain permission before using logos as links. Avoid using logos unless permission is given or obtained. Companies must and do protect the use of their logos. Some Web sites, such as search engines, promote having webmasters use their logos as links. They may even provide a selection of logos for that purpose. They may also have restrictions on how and where those logos may be used. Treat a logo as any other image. Read the fine print and keep a record of acceptable use.

5 Avoid linking to sites that are known to violate copyright laws.

▶ HTML

Hypertext Markup Language (HTML) tags are not copyrighted, but the design, text, and other content of a site are protected by copyright. With that in mind, it is acceptable to copy short passages of HTML under fair use, just as it is to copy a short passage from a larger work. Some code is "common knowledge" and not identifiable to any one Web site. Snipping a bit of code to generate a table or to position graphics is acceptable. It is not acceptable to copy a page's design without asking permission. If permission is granted, credit the original creator. Also, ask permission before copying anything beyond basic JavaScript or other forms of code.

▶ TAKING STEPS TO PROTECT THE SCHOOL DISTRICT AND WEB SITES

Much of this chapter has been about what constitutes copyright infringement. It is time to discuss some proactive steps regarding copyright. Districts can take measures to limit the district's liability in the event that an individual or group posts content on the Web that is in violation of copyright laws. There are also ways to protect Web sites from copyright violations. The plagiarism of educational Web sites is a problem faced by many educators.

A Safe Harbor for the District: Online Service Providers' Liability

The Digital Millennium Copyright Act (DMCA) has made it possible to limit the liability of online (Internet) service providers (OSPs or ISPs). The DMCA defines a service provider as an entity that transmits, routes, and connects users to online communications, or provides online or network services, such as storing digital material, caching, or providing location tools (directories, links,

FAST FACT

Though most copyright legal actions are civil, some infringements are criminal.

Penalties for breaking copyright can carry statutory fines, damages, or prison terms up to 10 years. Statutory fines start at $750 and can go to $30,000 for each violation. Offenders can be ordered to pay attorney fees and court costs. If offenders can prove themselves to be totally unknowledgeable, they are called "innocent infringers," and fines can be reduced to $200 per infringement. If violations are proven to be willful, deliberate, and informed, fines can be raised to $150,000 for each infringement. Liability is not limited to the offender. Employers, including nonprofit organizations and their administration, can be codefendants. Violations become felonies when the value of the item is over $2,500 and involves more than 10 copies. At the criminal level when infringement is deliberate and for profit or commercial purposes, individual fines can be $250,000, and organizational fines can be $500,000 per infringement. If a copyright protection system has been circumvented, organization fines can be as high as $1,000,000. At the criminal level, penalties can also include damages, court costs, and federal jail terms.

and so forth). A set of complicated requirements has to be met by an OSP to qualify for the protection afforded by the act. Libraries and educational institutions can qualify as OSPs and ISPs (Internet Service Providers). This safe harbor gives protection to the service providers if they have met all of the conditions of the Act. It does not protect individuals who are directly responsible for copyright infringements.

The Act specifies detailed procedures regarding the placement of materials online. Four restrictions that the OSP must follow to qualify for the limited liability are that the OSP may not do the following:

 RESOURCE BOX

ONLINE SERVICE PROVIDERS' LIABILITY

Lutzker, Lutzker, and Settlemyer have written a readable and authoritative summary of the OSP Liability Act.

Arnold P. Lutzker, et. al., *The Digital Millennium Copyright Act: Highlights of New Copyright Provision Establishing Limitation of Liability for Online Service Providers Executive Summary* <http://www.ala.org/washoff/osp.html> (November 18, 1998).

1 Place the material online

2 Create, choose, or change the material's content

3 Benefit financially because of the infringed materials

4 Know that the materials are in violation of copyright

In addition to meeting the criteria for the placement of the materials, the OSP also has to do the following:

5 Designate an individual to act as the OSP's copyright agent to handle notices about infringements

6 Register its copyright agent (name and address) with the copyright office <http://lcWeb.loc.gov/copyright/onlinesp/>

7 Create and post a copyright policy on the OSP's (district's or school's) Web site

8 Place the copyright agent's contact information on the OSP's (district's or school's) Web site

9 "Takedown" or disable offending materials if notified of an infringement

10 "Putback" materials within two weeks after receiving a "counter notice" if the dispute is not taken to the court system

11 Have a system capable of supporting the industry-standard technical measures taken by users to safeguard their materials from copyright violations and unauthorized usage

OSPs do not have to actively monitor use or materials, but must end privileges of users who infringe copyright.

Consult an attorney for additional information about Online Service Providers' Liability.

Protecting Web Sites

Some people truly do believe—mistakenly—that items on the Web are not protected by copyright. Although it may seem unlikely, school Web sites can be and are plagiarized. Copying a Web site's source code can be accomplished with a few mouse clicks. Entire educational Web sites have been and are being copied by other educators. Take the following simple steps to protect a Web site from being copied:

1 **DISPLAY A COPYRIGHT NOTICE:** Let users know that a site is copyrighted by putting a copyright notice with the word "copyright" or a ©, the date, and the author's/copyright holder's name at the bottom of each page. Write the words "All rights reserved." underneath the notice (including the period). The cost of registering a Web site is only $30. If it is possible that some day it might be necessary to prove ownership of a Web site and that the site is original work, it would be wise to register the site. If the site's original content is primarily text, use form TX. from the copyright Web site <http://lcweb.loc.gov/copyright/circs/circ66.pdf>. It is not necessary to re-register a site each time a change is made to the site. On his *Copyright on the Internet* Web site, <http://www.fplc.edu/tfield/cOpyNet.htm>, Thomas G. Field, Jr. makes the point,

> "While new text isn't covered by prior registrations, it is difficult to see why a court would allow someone to get away with copying a page of mostly registered content merely because it contains a few new sentences or other changes!"

2 **MAKE IMITATIONS EASY TO FIND:** A number of simple things can be done to make copies easy to find. Use search tools to search for deliberate clues that a plagiarist is likely to copy along with the rest of the Web site. Burying clues in a Web site can be as simple as putting unique text or an unusual link on some pages. Full-text search tools, such as *Google* <http://www.google.com> or *AltaVista* <http://www.altavista.com>, are great for finding the unique wordings, and both also can be used to search for links. Some Web authors intentionally misspell a couple of words and use full-text search engines to find copies. Think carefully before deliberately misspelling words on an educational Web site; it might reflect poorly on the school.

FAST FACT

It is possible to use JavaScript coding to deter users from opening the source code of a Web site.

META tags are also great tools for locating copies while increasing a site's visibility on the Web. Many search engines and tools search a Web site's META tags. For example, *Yahoo* <http://www.yahoo.com> searches META tags. The most important elements for search engines to be able to find are keywords and description META tags.

Make an image easier to find by giving it a unique name. Use search tools such as *HotBot* <http://www.hotbot.com> to search image names. Watermark software is available to "watermark" images. Watermark means that the images contain identifying bits of code that can be tracked if copied.

3 TAKE ACTION IF A SITE IS COPIED: While imitation is a form of flattery, it can also be a crime. Finding pages and pages of hard work copied without permission and without any due credit does feel like a form of theft. If finding that a site has been copied, remember that the individual making the copy may not be deliberately breaking the law. Even some professionals believe that the Internet is public domain or that "educational use" is a free license. The webmaster may be thinking that copying the Web site is the best way to meet students' needs. These specious rationales do not make copying acceptable, but being aware of them may help with preparing to make contact with the plagiarist, especially if the plagiarist was unknowledgeable about copyright laws.

Before contacting the webmaster, print copies of the offending pages and save copies of them to a hard drive. Write to the webmaster that the copies have been found. Be polite but firm with expectations. Explain that the copies violate the copyright laws and that virtually everything on the Web is protected by copyright. Tell infringers that the copied site needs to be removed from the Internet immediately. Indicate that they are welcome to link to your Web site. Remind them that copyright infringement carries serious legal consequences and that their administration and ISPs will be contacted if the situation is not resolved. Because many people do not read their e-mail daily, allow at least a week before contacting administrators. Phone calls may be necessary. Be prepared to demonstrate authorship and ownership of the Web site by showing copies of letters giving permission to link, the actual copyright registration information, dated early printouts from the Web, or whatever dated proof that can be produced. Know that having offending pages removed from the Internet may take weeks. **See** *Copyright Check Sheet* in **Appendix 1**.

▶ BEYOND FINES AND PENALTIES . . .

Why should educators be meticulous about copyright? Why should educators strain to read and understand what sounds like *Jabberwocky*? It is important to honor copyright on the Web as well as in our classrooms. If Web plagiarism is allowed to flourish unchecked, Web publishing may ultimately be discouraged. If Web authors find that they cannot safely post materials to the Web, many will begin to look for other ways to share their works.

The ultimate reason for being meticulous about copyright is students. Educators are role models, and students are watching. If students are involved in Web page publishing, they will see their teachers' careful efforts to honor the intellectual property rights of others. Even if students are merely utilizing the educational resources provided by the school Web site, they will see that credit has been given to intellectual property used in the construction of the site. When students see works acknowledged and attributed on school Web sites, they will know that giving credit is a priority. They may also better understand why they are expected to prepare bibliographies. If students are asked permission before their work is posted to the Internet, they will see that educators are serious about not copying without permission. How educators handle copyright on educational Web sites may be one of the best opportunities to teach students about copyright and the ethical use of information.

 RESOURCE BOX

CANADIAN COPYRIGHT LINKS

Canadian Library Association (CLA), Resources—Copyright Information
<http://www.cla.ca/resources/copyrigt.htm>
CLA offers this online handbook of resources covering Canadian and international copyright legislation.

CANCOPY
<http://www.cancopy.com/welcome.shtml>
This is the official Web site of the Canadian Copyright Licensing Agency. This site provides information for copyright owners and users.

Department of Justice, Consolidated Statutes and Regulations: Copyright Act
http://canada.justice.gc.ca/en/laws/C-42/index.html
Here is a consolidated version of the Copyright Act posted by the Department of Justice, Canada.

Carriere, Laurent, Fair Dealing in Canada
<http://www.robic.ca/publications/032e.htm>
"This document is designed to familiarize the reader with matters of general interest relating to intellectual property law."

Government of Canada, Parliamentary Business and Publications
<http://www.parl.gc.ca/bills/government/C-32/C-32_3/12472b-3E.html#20>
Section of Bill C-32 as passed by the House of Commons is on this Web site. It explains the concept of "fair dealing" as an exception in copyright infringement.

Harris, Lesley Ellen, Copyright Law & Libraries, Archives & Museums
<http://www.mcgrawhill.ca/copyrightlaw/cllib.html>
Harris provides a comprehensive look at Canadian copyright law as it pertains to libraries, museums, and archival collections.

Harris, Lesley Ellen, Copyrightlaws.com
<http://www.copyrightlaws.com/>
This is "an informative Web site devoted to international copyright law, digital property, media and other intellectual property issues."

Industry Canada, Canadian Intellectual Property Office, Copyrights
<http://strategis.ic.gc.ca/sc_mrksv/cipo/cp/cp_main-e.html>
This site includes FAQ, legislation, and guides to electronic document delivery and registration surrounding copyright.

CANADIAN COPYRIGHT LINKS continued

MaLaughlin, Jeff, Intellectual Property and the New Media
<http://www.cariboo.bc.ca/ae/php/phil/mclaughl/ppt/copyright/sld001.htm>
This online presentation discusses copyright law and the Internet.

Manitoba Education, Canadian Copyright Information
<http://www.edu.gov.mb.ca/metks4/instruct/iru/pubs/web/c/index.html>
Here is a collection of links to Web sites that contain information about Canadian copyright law.

Manitoba Education, Interpretations of Canadian Copyright Law
<http://www.edu.gov.mb.ca/metks4/instruct/iru/pubs/web/c/index.html#interpret>
This section from the previous collection is devoted specifically to sites that interpret Canadian copyright law.

Stohn, Stephen, Overview of Canadian Copyright
<http://www.stohnhenderson.com/articles/overview.html>
A Canadian lawyer created this overview of Canadian copyright.

Sotiriadis, Bob H., A Summary of Some Distinctions Between Canadian and American Copyright Law and Practice
<http://www.robic.ca/publications/228.htm>
Written by a Canadian lawyer, this article compares Canadian and American copyright laws.

Telus Learning Connection, What Every Teacher Should Know About Copyright
<http://www.2learn.ca/copyright/gencopyright.html>
This Web bibliography of sites deals with Canadian copyright facts and issues. It is geared specifically toward teachers.

Chapter 6

Gathering Resources... Just Who Is Needed?

Talent wins games, but teamwork and intelligence win championships.

—Michael Jordan

O nce the decisions are made about why a Web site is being created and to whom the information is targeted, make certain that the people resources are in place to support a Web site. Many schools that have gone ahead and built Web sites without taking this step have been surprised to discover how many administrative and technical issues they need to handle. Managing reactively takes an enormous amount of work. It is much better to "get your ducks in a row" before issues arise.

Never build a school Web site in isolation from the school or district administration. Many of the responsibilities for owning and maintaining a Web site require the authority to act on behalf of the school or district, and in many cases school districts already have people or processes in place to handle the details. Find out what needs to be managed, what is already taken care of, and who is responsible for what. Then pull people into Web teams that can guide the entire process on an ongoing basis. **See** *Technical Support Resource List* in **Appendix 1**.

⊳ WHO'S IN CHARGE HERE?

The first step in organizing the administrative end of school Web publishing endeavors is to clarify and assign responsibility. Putting together a Web site using Hypertext Markup Language (HTML) or one of the many authoring tools on the market is quite simple. But before that process even begins, a school must address who is responsible—not just for the building of the site, but also for all the details that go with it. A look at the administrative questions that need to be handled for a school Web site will reveal the number and variety of people involved. Once selected, these individuals will become members of school and district Web teams that oversee the school and district Web sites. Some of the administrative questions that need to be addressed include the following:

1 Who is responsible for maintaining the Web server(s)?

2 Whom do schools contact for help?

3 Who is responsible for training the developers and end users?

4 Who are the contacts for security issues?

5 Who is responsible for creating, reviewing, and revising guidelines?

6 Who is responsible for content?

7 Who fields complaints about the site from outside the organization?

8 Who is permitted to upload to the server(s)?

9 How will the district communicate to schools regarding changes?

10 How will the Web teams be structured?

While clarifying these issues, keep in mind that often two levels handle aspects of each issue: a district or school board level and a local or school level. These levels will overlap in some areas. Those schools that are not part of a district (some private, charter, or other special schools) or are in small districts will find that they must contend with both categories of issues. Much of what needs to be dealt with just takes some organization and is not difficult. Not taking the time to organize before creating the site will cost valuable time later. In a perfect world, schools have access to all the individuals or groups listed in the following sections; however, in reality often only a few people wearing many hats are responsible for these tasks. No matter how many people end up with responsibilities, it is essential that they work collaboratively toward a common vision and purpose and try to be flexible while they fulfill their roles.

WHO IS RESPONSIBLE FOR THE WEB SERVER(S)?

Who should be responsible for the Web server depends on where the school Web site will be hosted. If the school district has its own Web servers, the site will likely reside on those servers. If the school decides to operate its own Web server, the site will be hosted locally on that server. If neither of these is an option, schools can still take advantage of one of the many public servers on the Internet that provide space for Web sites, sometimes for free. Specialized online services are available that provide "fill-in-the-box" forms for automatically generating school or classroom Web pages. These require little expertise but produce practical pages that can be used right away. Whether schools have a district server or local server, or use a publicly available service, someone needs to have an understanding of the host in use. This can be as simple as knowing where and how to upload or as complex as how to run a local server. But it all begins with knowing where the Web site is hosted.

District Servers

At the district level, a technology department usually carries responsibility for some aspects and decisions of all school Web sites for the district. Schools that have the support of this department should count themselves lucky, as they can concentrate directly on their school Web sites and leave the technical and server responsibilities to the technology group. For a technology department, many of these responsibilities easily blend with procedures and practices already in place. Some of these responsibilities may include the following:

1 Housing the Web servers

2 Configuring the servers

3 Overseeing the connections to the Internet

4 Upgrading server software and hardware

5 Programming for special Web applications (Java, databases, and so forth)

6 Investigating and implementing new Web technologies (streaming media, secure transactions, and so forth)

7 Monitoring usage and providing reports

8 Troubleshooting the Web servers

9 Making decisions about and documenting surrounding structure and conventions (**see Chapter 7** on *Technical Considerations* for examples)

10 Providing district-wide communication avenues (chats, mailing lists, and so forth)

11 Communicating policy and procedure surrounding Web site development

> **FAST FACT**
>
> Fast Fact: Server documentation is a written record of technical information and special settings for the server.

> **QUICK TIP**
>
> If the school has no technical support staff, it is difficult and unrealistic to add this additional burden to teaching or support staff. If schools intend to run Web servers locally, they should consider adding technical staff to maintain them or providing plenty of release time for the staff member responsible.

School-Based Servers

Schools that operate without a technology department and wish to run their own server face the previously mentioned responsibilities locally. The same is true if the school intends to run a local Intranet server of information available only within the school. Someone must be dedicated to work with and learn about the local server. The person responsible for the local server must prepare and maintain documentation to go with it. If the local server administrator is unavailable for any length of time, the documentation ensures that another person can assume that role without compromising the Web site or needing to deconstruct or guess at the procedures for running the system.

Public Servers

If the school Web site resides on one of the many public spaces available on the Internet, there is less need to worry about server issues previously mentioned because the Internet Service Provider (ISP) or Application Service Provider (ASP) will be taking care of them. Instead, someone needs to investigate and evaluate the services offered by different providers to find the hosting package that is appropri-

> **QUICK TIP**
>
> Every server has idiosyncrasies, and someone in the school should be familiar with the server the school is using. This person should be available for technical support and should be the one who contacts the district technical department, ISP, or ASP if the server does not seem to be performing properly.

FREE HOSTING SERVICES

Angelfire and Geocities are two popular hosting services where free Web space is available, but beware—a number of Internet filtering products block both services.

<http://www.angelfire.com/>
<http://www.geocities.com/>

SCHOOL WEB PAGE GENERATION SERVICES

AMERICAN SCHOOL DIRECTORY
<http://www.asd2.com/resources/introduction.html>
This is another service that generates and hosts school Web sites online.

COPERNICUS EDUCATION GATEWAY: SCHOOLNOTES
<http://www.schoolnotes.com/>
This site generates and hosts individual Web pages for posting school information or assignments online.

FILAMENTALITY
<http://www.kn.pacbell.com/wired/fil>
Fill in the Filamentality blanks to generate and host a subject resource page online.

HIGHWIRED.COM
<http://www.highwired.com/>
This site provides services that include an online class management system, generated school and personal Web pages, and e-mail and group messaging.

TEACHER WEB
<http://teacherweb.com/>
This free service allows teachers to generate a classroom Web site by filling in forms and selecting colors, graphics, and buttons.

TEACHERS.NET HOME PAGE MAKER
<http://teachers.net/sampler/>
Here is a simple, Web-based form that generates an HTML page upon submission. The code is then e-mailed to the creator for uploading on the school Web site.

WEBADEMIC.COM
<http://www.webAdemic.com/>
This site provides a service for generating and hosting specialized pages for school Web sites including, homework pages, calendars, news, and handbook pages.

ate for the school. An ISP can provide access to the Internet and Web space on the server to host school Web pages. An ASP may provide space, build and maintain the site, and often have additional services available. Once the host server is selected, someone locally who is good with technology still needs to dedicate some time to learning the requirements of the host server.

➤ WHOM DO SCHOOLS CONTACT FOR HELP?

Working on a Web site generates all kinds of questions—not only "How do we . . .?" but also "Can we . . .?" Many new ideas and questions will blossom as the school Web site is built. As with any technology, a support mechanism must be in place to help with development and implementation. This support mechanism can include district support specialists and local support specialists.

District Support Specialists

Ideally the school board or district will have an individual or group that is familiar with the district policies, procedures, and server environment. This group can provide invaluable assistance to school Web authors and administrators. Schools will always have questions about what they can do on their Web pages, and someone has to be able to answer them with a perspective of the "big picture." In some school districts, the support will come from a technology coordinator, a specialist, or a technician. A help desk may provide support. The help desk

> **QUICK TIP**
>
> Keep a list of the primary contact people for questions about the school Web site near the phone in the office, the library media center, the computer lab, and any other location where staff may need it. This information will speed up processes and help staff know who is responsible for what.

may also dictate how much and what type of support is provided. This group or individual must be aware of current Internet technologies, what is possible, and what is permitted on the district servers.

The district support specialist(s) must also be familiar with the environment within the schools and the tools being used. They should be comfortable with the tools even if they are not masters of every one of them. They need to continually review what is being used and suggest upgrades when necessary.

Local Support Specialists

Often, schools will experiment with tools and technologies that are specific to the classroom or project, and the help desk may not be able to assist them for a variety of reasons. In this case, one or more individuals to serve as a local support persons within the school are invaluable. These people must be comfortable working with Web sites, keep up with related news and issues in Web development, and have a good understanding of the policies and procedures for the district. They are the primary points of contact within the school. If the school is running a local Web server, the local support specialist(s) will need a much higher level of technical expertise than if the server is located at the district or with an external ISP.

Local support specialists are often teachers, librarians/media specialists, or technology coordinators in the school. These individuals have many responsibilities besides managing the school Web site. Those within the school should know who these people are and when they are available for general assistance versus an emergency. If no guidelines cover availability, the local support specialists will be inundated with requests for assistance while they are trying to manage all their other responsibilities.

The local support specialists should be able to deal with many issues related to Web pages. They may need to test or suggest new technologies for the school Web site or for classroom projects. They will be highly involved with the school Web team, if not leading it, and will be able to field the most common questions about Web site development for the school. They are the ones to whom school staff direct questions about Web development, and they escalate questions to the district level, ISP, or ASP, if required.

Figure 6.1 Deb Logan's Web Page Tutorial

<http://www.deblogan.com/ design.html>
This site was created by one of the authors to help school and library webmasters learn to build high quality sites. This set of tutorials was created for use as online, self-paced study or as a complement to instructor-led sessions. *Deb Logan, Mount Gilead, Ohio*

Responsibility for Training

Training is always a hot potato within schools and school districts. Who provides the training? Will it be offered as instructor-led training or as self-paced, computer-based training? How will release or substitute time be covered? Will it be during school hours or after hours? Who pays for it? Many questions need resolution in the area of training. By working together, schools and districts can find ways to support training opportunities for staff who are responsible for the school and district Web pages. The key is to be creative and cooperative while understanding that the costs may need to be shared among schools, districts, and individuals. Ultimately, each of those stakeholders will directly benefit from the training.

Training developed and presented by internal staff has the advantage of being specific to the school or district. The challenge for some schools and districts is whether there are internal staff members who have the time and expertise to develop, present, monitor, and maintain the training. If time or expertise is an issue, contract external training providers. These organizations often have the expertise, but may lack an understanding of the local or educational environment. When external training providers are contracted, it is essential that they work closely with the school or district throughout the project. The training provider should be flexible and sensitive to any special needs of the environment. Schools and districts must be clear about their needs and communicate them to the training provider early in the planning process.

What type of training will be offered? Instructor-led, hands-on training provides the advantage of human interaction and immediate assistance. Classroom sessions outside the school allow participants to focus on the topics at hand without the distraction of other tasks. Attending classroom sessions can be a challenge for many, however, because of the added cost of providing substitute or release time. Organizing travel can be problematic if the courses are held at a remote location.

One answer to the issues surrounding instructor-led training is to provide some form of computer-based instruction. This could be in the form of CBT (computer-based training) modules on CD-ROM, disks, or a shared network. It may be in the form of WBT

Figure 6.2 Montgomery County Public Schools—WebSmarts

<http://www.mcps.k12.md.us/departments/isa/ resources/grants/welcomewebsmarts.html>
WebSmarts is an online training program in electronic literacy to help teachers integrate technology into classroom practice. It was developed for MCPS teachers and made available from the district Web site. *Aimee Timmins and Nancy Carey, MCPS Research and Development Team, Montgomery County Public Schools, Rockville, Maryland*

A DISTRICT CASE STUDY

In 1996, the Calgary Public Board of Education (CBE) began examining how it was going to manage its school Web sites. In a district of over 98,000 students in over 240 schools, the district could not possibly create and maintain the Web sites for the schools, nor did it believe it should. Instead, the district created a basic profile for each school, but individual school Web sites were optional. Schools that wanted a site would have to build their own, and the Internet Support Team became the springboard to help them.

To enable schools with the project, the Internet Support Team created the Web Administrator Training Program. Developed internally, the program consisted of a full range of Internet and Web publishing courses to help staff become familiar with the variety of tools and opportunities afforded by using the Web in education and specifically within CBE. Schools selected two individuals from their staff to become the Web Administrators. Although no restrictions dictated selection of staff, the recommendation was that one of the two Web Administrators be a classroom teacher. These Web Administrators served as the central point of contact for the district and received training and support through the district Internet Support Team.

The training program had four components and was four-and-a-half days long. Due to the problems associated with staff being out of the school for that length of time, each component was complete in itself and was offered once a month. This format allowed Web Administrators to take the courses as the need or interest arose and with as little disruption to the school as possible. The four components of the program were Internet Fundamentals, Web Publishing, Managing Student Internet Access, and Integrating the Internet into the Classroom. The district covered the cost of trainers, a training lab, the training materials, and ongoing support by means of the Internet Support Team. Schools covered the substitute or release time that would enable their Web Administrators to attend the training.

Supporting Web Publishing

A complete set of online HTML tutorials was developed to walk staff through the process of creating Web pages. These were made available to everyone in the district (not just the Web Administrators) and could be done as self-paced units whenever convenient. Some sections were used within the Web Administrator training program itself, and the tutorials were continuously updated as HTML evolved with the Web. Permission to upload school Web pages was granted once the school had at least one Web Administrator who had completed the Web Publishing section of the Web Administrator Training Program.

The Web Publishing section of the program covered Web page design, construction techniques, and hands-on construction using HTML. Because schools could select their own authoring tools, the pros and cons of authoring tools were discussed in the program, but instruction with specific tools was not provided. There were also modules that covered the CBE Publishing Guidelines and permission forms required, special features and tools available (such as counters and forms), and any internal requirements when working with CBE servers.

In 1999, a second optional day of Web publishing training was added to cover intermediate Web publishing techniques and to provide additional support through facilitated working time. The facilitated working time allowed the Web Administrators an opportunity to work directly on their school sites with a member of the Internet Support Team on hand to answer questions about construction, guidelines, or other development issues.

Communication and Ongoing Support

An internal Web Administrator mailing list facilitated communication between the district and the Web Administrators. A Web-enabled database provided quick access to contact information for all other Web Administrators within CBE for additional networking and support. The HTML tutorials and training modules were continually updated as part of the Web Administrator training program. Did it work? From 1997 to 1999, close to 60 schools launched their own school sites, and a number of special project sites were posted to the CBE project server.

(Web-based training) available through the Internet or a school or district Intranet. Computer-based instruction allows staff to receive training at their convenience and often from their own location. Challenges with computer-based instruction include accommodating the different technological skill levels of participants (because they may not have immediate assistance when taking the course), self-motivation and discipline to participate, assessment and accountability, and the ever-present difficulty of finding the time. Although time is an issue no matter what type of delivery method is chosen, computer-based instruction is usually coupled with an expectation that staff will complete it on their own time, an expectation that is unrealistic and unfair to staff.

Issues surrounding costs and who pays for the training also need to be addressed. Creating a training program, whether in-house or contracted through a vendor, requires development and delivery costs. Maintaining the program and keeping it current generate continual costs—rarely is training a one-shot deal. Technology advances and staff turnover create a need for ongoing commitment to training. Some schools and districts cover the cost of staff development, viewing it as an investment to help ensure quality teaching and learning. Other districts direct staff to opportunities but do not pay for courses, viewing them as personal development with little gain to the district. More often, schools and districts (often in conjunction with professional organizations) share the cost of staff development, believing that they also share the benefits.

▶ RESPONSIBILITY FOR SECURITY

Some security issues can be dealt with through the technology (settings on servers and other hardware), while others may be managed through policy (**see Chapter 3**, *Blueprints for a Firm Foundation: Publishing Guidelines and Policies*). Regardless of the means of handling security issues, people are ultimately responsible for making the decisions. These people must be available as contacts in the event of a problem. The kind of security issues that may confront schools include the following:

1. Hackers interfering with or disabling the servers
2. Students or staff snooping through the internal network or system
3. Inappropriate or illegal copying of school sites or files
4. Posting of inappropriate content
5. Posting of scripts or files that compromise security
6. Unsafe posting of personal information
7. Public availability of internal/sensitive information
8. Censorship issues surrounding posted content

At the district level, a security advisor is needed. A security advisor is an individual or group who manages security issues surrounding the use of the district servers. Security advisors are familiar with the many legal and privacy issues confronting educational use of the Internet. They work with those responsible for the technology to ensure that appropriate security measures are in place on school and district hardware. Schools and the public contact this person or group with concerns, problems, or issues. Security advisors are also major contributors to Web publishing policies and guidelines for the school or district.

Locally, schools need to have someone who is accessible to staff, students, and parents in order to address questions and concerns surrounding security issues on the school Web site. Again, this is often a teacher, a librarian, or a technology coordinator. This person needs to be familiar with the guidelines and recommendations of the district. It is important that this person knows whom to contact in the event of a problem or issue that the person is unable to resolve.

A school usually has many authors working on its school site, and adherence to the guidelines needs to be checked before posting pages. A local Web team coordinator may handle this at the school level. If the school is part of a district, someone from the district level might also check for compliance.

▶ RESPONSIBILITY FOR POLICY & GUIDELINES

If the school is part of a district, a district-level team or committee should work on policies and guidelines—not just once, but regularly. This team is extremely important, and although it resides at the district level, it must be composed of members from various schools and departments. The decisions of this group become part of the general Web policies and guidelines for all the schools within the district.

The Internet continually changes, and guidelines that were appropriate two years ago may no longer be suitable. Consequently, this group needs to constantly review the current state of Web use in education. A review schedule should be in place so this essential task is not overlooked each year. Policies and guidelines created by this group should be broad enough to accommodate the variety of uses required of the site(s), while still providing structure and direction to school Web authors.

Individual schools may also want to have someone responsible for overseeing local guidelines—this may fall to the local Web team. For example, teachers may put a limit on the size or number of graphics used for a specific project, or the school may decide that all the newsletters for the school will be in a specific format. Local guidelines are only to fine-tune the local school site; they do not replace district guidelines.

▶ RESPONSIBILITY FOR CONTENT

Although there is no shortage of content that could be put on a school Web site, the vision and purpose will guide decisions as to exactly what does belong on the site. Chapter 3, *What Goes on an Educational Web Site?*, provides numerous possibilities for content, but someone needs to decide what is appropriate. An individual or group should develop content guidelines that are flexible enough to accommodate the diversity within the district and to clarify when additional approval is needed. The content created at the district level differs greatly from that of a local school, and this group or individual works with the guidelines as to what is appropriate.

District-level content is usually administrative and is created by district-level staff or converted from existing school district documents. It is sometimes created by a communications department and run through a legal department to ensure "media sensitivity" prior to being posted for public consumption. District-level materials are politically sensitive and must be handled with care. Someone should be the "sober second thought" that all administrative pages go through prior to being uploaded for the district because the school board is liable for the material it posts on the Web site.

School-based content can have much greater flexibility, variety, and flair. Although teachers or support staff

> **QUICK TIP**
>
> With so much variety in content being published on a school Web site, schools must be ready to face content challenges/censorship attempts.
>
> Make certain that district policies and procedures on materials selection and challenge are updated to provide effective guidance for dealing with digital resources and issues.
>
> Librarians are especially adept at managing content challenges and can help ensure that intellectual freedom is maintained while responding to the challenges.

may create the administrative pages for the school, students are often the creators of material at the school level. The topics of student Web pages may be as diverse as are the students. Topics can range from the practical to the absurd, but student Web pages are worthy of publishing if the quality of writing is good and the content appropriate. In some cases, school districts may permit outside organizations or volunteers to contribute content. In these cases, these groups need additional guidance as to what information will be allowed on the school Web site.

The importance of keeping an eye on content becomes evident in "Implementing and Managing Web Site Development in Education" (Alberta Education, 1999, available at <http://www.learning.gov.ab.ca/ technology/bestpractices/pdf/websitedevelopment.pdf>), which states, ". . . in Web publishing, the damages resulting from malicious publishing may far exceed those formerly associated with school newspapers." Copyright regulations need to be clearly spelled out for students and staff, and Web contributors must be held accountable for adhering to those rules. Schools are also liable for what they post, so again, a double check of all content before publishing is necessary. Chapter 4, *Blueprints for a Firm Foundation: Publishing Guidelines and Policies,* and Chapter 5, *Copyright Issues and the Web,* discuss additional details surrounding liability issues and the application of the Digital Millennium Copyright Act for educational environments.

Occasionally, content on the school Web site generates complaints. Individuals assigned to monitor content should work closely with the school librarian and keep the security team informed if censorship issues arise.

▶ RESPONSIBILITY FOR UPLOADING

One of the big questions that faces schools is "Who is allowed to upload on the server?" The answer: the fewer, the better. The school or district Web site is the school's face to the world. Schools are liable for what goes on the site and must exercise control over it. Uploading should be the responsibility of specific staff members and should never be left to students or volunteers. This is *especially* true if the school is part of a larger network as other schools or systems can be compromised.

Some school districts will do all the uploading for their schools. This step increases the safety of the server and can help with maintaining quality control and consistency. It does, however, create an enormous workload and rob schools of the ability to make quick changes to their own Web sites. Other schools or districts permit numerous people to upload school pages. This policy does reduce the initial workload for the district, but it can seriously increase the security risk and reduce the overall quality of the Web site.

Beware of parents or students who volunteer to create and host the site on their personal ISP; schools have been caught in a trap on finding that the information produced was not appropriate and the school could not change it. In some cases, schools have had the student or parent move away, leaving the site inaccessible to the school. Web sites created by students or parents in such cases do not belong to the school, but to the creator, and that creator makes the decision to change the pages.

Schools have had servers and networks corrupted or hacked because students uploaded inappropriate or dangerous files and programs. Volunteers have posted information that put staff and students at risk or that did not reflect the opinions or policies of the school or district. If schools use students or volunteers in the process, ensure that a staff member always has the current password to get in, and screen all files before uploading.

▷ RESPONSIBILITY FOR GROWTH AND FUTURE PLANNING

A school district should have a plan for coordinating the district's school Web sites. With the number of people who may be involved, school districts need reliable communication channels to facilitate the flow of information throughout the system. Mailing lists or discussion forums, regular meetings, and regular communications in the form of newsletters or bulletins designed for school webmasters are essential to this function, but they need to be managed by someone.

The plan should also recognize and provide for changes in personnel and students. Every six to twelve months, an individual or group at both the district level and the school level needs to revisit the status of those who are assigned responsibility to see whether they are still available and able to participate. Each year will bring new staff, new students, and new volunteers into the picture. The people responsible for the Web site one year may be different the next, but longevity can be built in by assigning responsibility to positions rather than to specific individuals. Each year the teams need to review their progress and evaluate their goals to ensure they are still on the right track with their site.

▷ CREATING WEB TEAMS

Web teams are essential to thriving, long-term school Web sites. Without knowing it, most schools and districts already have individuals doing the work of a Web team, but the individuals may not be communicating with one another. Sometimes it is simply a matter of pulling them together and formalizing the team so all of them can share what they are doing. **See** *District Web Planning Team Information Sheet* or *School Web Planning Team Information Sheet* in **Appendix 1.**

At the district level, school boards usually have a formal group in place that can manage all the responsibilities outlined earlier in this chapter and that can communicate the information to the schools. Because this team deals with many policy and procedural issues, a good mix of members includes the following:

1. District-level administrator
2. School board trustee
3. School principal
4. Librarian/media specialist and library technician

FAST FACT

There are many reasons to invite school librarians/media specialists to be members of educational Web teams.

They have specialized training that can be invaluable in the creation of online resources. Some of the unique assets that school librarians/media specialists potentially bring to Web teams include the following:

1. **Knowledge of the school's curriculum:** Because many librarians/media specialists form instructional partnerships with their building's staff members, they often have the best overview of who teaches what and when across a building's grade levels. This knowledge can be used to develop online curriculum resource collections for teachers and students.

2. **Expertise in the selection of resources:** A major component in the training and education of librarians/media specialists is how to evaluate and select educational materials. This can be helpful in locating quality resources for Web pages. Librarians/media specialists can train others to select materials.

3. **Experience with writing annotations:** Librarians/media specialists are taught to write meaningful annotations about resources. Links on Web sites should be annotated.

4. **Training in organizing resources with an awareness of accessibility:** Making resources available is a required element of librarians'/media specialists' educational programs. They are taught to classify and organize materials in a way that users will be able to locate and use them. The contents of educational Web sites need to be organized with accessibility in mind.

5. **Knowledge about copyright:** Frequently, librarians/media specialists are the best informed members of a school district on the subject of copyright. Copyright is often confusing, and there are many misconceptions about copyright and the Web.

6. **Leadership in Technology:** Librarians/media specialists are often among the most technologically sophisticated members of an educational staff.

5 Teacher

6 District-level computer/server technician

7 School-based computer technician or technology coordinator

8 Security/legal advisor

9 Public or media relations department representative

10 Parent

One person should be responsible for coordinating the district Web team and making certain that information and changes in policy or procedure get to the Web team coordinators in the schools. Individual schools should have a Web team coordinator who manages issues locally and communicates within the school. School Web teams deal primarily with construction, content, and local software issues, so a good mix for this team would include the following:

1 School principal

2 Librarian/media specialist

3 Teacher

4 Computer technician or technology coordinator

5 Parent

6 Community member

7 Students

The Web team coordinator clarifies who leads and who follows. The coordinator usually is also responsible for encouraging and supporting teachers to create special Web-based projects, communicating with members of the district Web team, assigning responsibility among the team members, networking with other school webmasters, and uploading pages. This person also checks that pages follow the approved content, design, and technical guidelines.

Schools might need to have someone to work with graphics, someone to create or gather content, and someone to discern the overall structure of the site and how to add and take pieces out of it effectively. Schools may need someone who can write scripts for special functionality, such as connecting with a database or processing forms.

In reality, school Web teams probably do not have all of these members; however, it never hurts to go for the best possible scenario. Trying to have everyone represented gives a much better picture of what can and should be done with the school Web site, and a much faster response time when things go wrong.

The Web team members need to have some basic training, not only to build the pages but also to adhere to school Web publishing guidelines and work within the technical environment. They need to be kept apprised of changes in policy. The team needs to understand that what they publish affects the school, the district, members of the community, and individuals at the school.

School Web teams should meet regularly to discuss information about the school that might belong on the Web site, to brainstorm for changes and growth, to answer questions as they arise, and to find out if anyone on the team needs assistance. Like any other extracurricular activity, the school Web team is an excellent place for students to develop a host of real-life skills.

School and district Web teams are part of the administrative chain for managing the school Web site. Members need to have the authority to act on their assigned responsibilities, to remedy a problem that falls under their jurisdiction, or to directly contact the person who can take action. The decisions of members of the Web teams often become part of the Web Publishing Policies and Guidelines for the school or district. Due to the role these team members play, it is wise for them to have an understanding of the technical issues involved with a Web site to assist them with these decisions. (Chapter 7, *Technical Considerations*, will help identify and address these issues.) These teams, along with the policies and guidelines, direct the work of Web authors throughout the district and provide an essential support mechanism for school and district Web sites.

RESOURCE BOX

WEB TEAM RESOURCE BOX

School Web Clubs
<http://supportnet.merit.edu/webclubs/index.html>
This is a collection of resources for creating and supporting student Web clubs.

The Web Team: What's Best—Centralized or Decentralized Web Staffing?
<http://www.electronic-school.com/0698f4.html>
This article discusses managerial/staffing aspects for school Web sites.

Chapter 7

Technical Considerations

Any sufficiently advanced technology is indistinguishable from magic.

—*Arthur C. Clarke*

E xamining the technical environment of the school or district Web site is an important part of the process for creating or managing the site. Schools need to select a server for their Web site and to learn the technical requirements surrounding the server. It is easy enough to build a Web site, but building without knowing the technical requirements can generate plenty of repair work later. As the technical considerations are defined or discovered, many of them become part of the publishing guidelines that direct the work of the Web authors. **See** *Technical Considerations & Constraints Check Sheet* in **Appendix 1**.

Most districts already have many of the issues covered by the technical structure that is already in place (server hardware and software, network capabilities and restrictions, connectivity, and so forth). In these cases, the district technical structure defines how and where the Web sites for the schools fit and the specifications that must be followed. Schools that are running their own servers make these decisions locally, then communicate the requirements to their local Web authors. Schools that house their school Web site on a public server or with one of the many educational portals on the Internet need to get the technical information from the provider they are using, then share what is necessary with local Web authors.

Technical issues that may need to be clarified include the following:

1 Where will the site be hosted?

2 Which authoring tool(s) should be used?

3 Which maintenance tool(s) should be used?

4 How will the usage of the site be tracked?

5 How much space does the school have on the server?

6 How should the files and folders be organized?

7 What naming conventions must be followed?

8 How will pages and sites be uploaded?

9 Are there any restrictions surrounding what can be loaded?

10 Who is permitted to upload?

11 How should pages and sites be linked within the server?

12 What are the guidelines surrounding the removal of pages or sites?

13 What scripts are available for use?

14 Can changes be made and tested before going live?

➤ FINDING A HOME OF YOUR OWN: WHERE WILL THE SITE BE HOSTED?

The decision regarding where the site ultimately resides on the Internet guides almost all other technical considerations. Selecting a home for the school Web site depends a great deal on what the school district has available and policies surrounding the publishing of school information.

If the school board or district has Web servers available, the school site probably will be located on those servers and will be governed by that technical environment. When this is the case, schools need to keep in mind that the restrictions of that technical environment are not made arbitrarily. Restrictions are the result of the hardware and software in use and the layout and security policies of the district network. Restrictions also look at the impact that Web site building has on the entire district.

Schools that decide to run their own Web server may house their site locally and create it according to the technical environment they define. They have more autonomy and technical control over their site and what they can do with it, but they also incur the costs associated with purchasing, maintaining, and upgrading the server hardware and software.

Schools that wish to run their own servers when they are part of a school district have additional points to consider. Much of their publishing is still governed by the guidelines and policies of the district of which they are a part. These schools can also pose security threats to the district network, depending on the setup of their local server. Some schools have set up their own Web servers and configured them so students can dial in from home to use the system. Although this may be an excellent method of enabling student access, it is a direct threat to the school network if a server that allows dial-up connections is also connected to a larger district network. Allowing these external connections creates a direct security violation that can compromise the entire system. Schools that are part of a district network and that wish to run their own Web servers must collaborate with the district technology department before considering such an initiative.

FAST FACT

Schools that gather all the technical details from the district prior to building Web sites and work within the confines of the environment provided will have fewer surprises and much greater success with the Web site they produce.

With the variety of easy-to-use Web server software on the market, it is not unrealistic for schools to run their own server. To do so, schools need to dedicate at least one powerful computer as the Web server and install and configure Web server software on it. Although any powerful desktop computer can be set up as a server, the performance will be well below that of server hardware and

SERVER INFORMATION

Apache Web Server
<http://httpd.apache.org/>
This is the official site of the Apache Server Project.

IBM WebSphere
<http://www-4.ibm.com/software/webservers/>
This is the official site for IBM Web server information.

Macintosh WebStar Server
<http://www.starnine.com/>
This is the official site of the WebStar server suite for the Macintosh platform.

Microsoft Internet Information Server
<http://www.microsoft.com/technet/iis/>
This site houses a large collection of resources and technical notes to support Internet Information Server (IIS) from Microsoft.

Netscape Server Products
<http://home.netscape.com/servers/>
This is the official site for Netscape server products.

Server Watch: Web Servers
<http://serverwatch.internet.com/webservers.html>
This site presents technical information covering numerous types of Web servers.

Serving Up Web Server Basics—How a Web Server Works
<http://webcompare.internet.com/webbasics/index.html>
This is an in-depth tutorial explaining how a Web server works and how to choose a platform. It also discusses security issues and configurations.

Web Server Compare: The Definitive Guide to HTTP Server Specs
<http://webcompare.internet.com/>
This site houses technical information, reviews, and comparisons covering a variety of Web servers.

is not recommended. In addition, keep in mind that configuring and securing the server requires technical expertise, and maintaining the server requires a great deal of time.

If the site will be located on one of the public servers or educational portals on the Internet, the technical specifications of that server will guide the Web page work of the school. Someone at the school (usually the Web team coordinator) should be familiar with the technical requirements of the hosting server before pages are created. Chapter 6, *Gathering Resources . . .Just Who Is Needed?,* includes a list of hosting services for school Web pages.

▶ SELECTING SOFTWARE TOOLS

The boom in Web authoring and Web maintenance software has created a plethora of options for Web authors and administrators. These tools are an essential part of Web authoring, and sites that are not incorporating the incredible capabilities available with these tools are not just missing out, they are creating more work for themselves.

School Web authors need to have a collection of goodies, including tools for Web authoring, graphics and compression, site management, and maintenance. Syntax checkers, link checkers, special spell checkers, and statistics reporting are just a few of the maintenance tools. Some of these tools can be downloaded free, bought outright, or purchased by subscription from the Web. (A list of tools is included in **Appendix 2.**) In all cases, first see whether the school board or district provides any of the tools or has defined a standard for the district that should govern what is purchased. Second, select software for use at the school.

Authoring Tools

Web authoring tools generate code automatically, allowing authors to create Web pages without writing the code by hand. When it comes to authoring tools, the problem is that not all tools are created equal. Some are proprietary, and some of the features they create will work only on specific servers. Some create pages that are best viewed with only certain versions of Web browsers. Some are easy to use on a local computer but need special configurations or fine-tuning to create pages that will work on the server. What all of this means is buyer beware. Before purchasing a Web authoring tool, get a demo and try it. Make sure the server being used will support any special features the school wants to use. This is especially important when integrating databases, using interactive forms, and adding rotating banners or other specialized functions.

> **FAST FACT**
>
> A piece of software for making Web pages is referred to as a *Web editor* or a *Web authoring tool.*
>
> Instead of using a Web editor, some webmasters write their pages using code. The most commonly used code for building Web pages at this time is called HTML. HTML stands for Hypertext Markup Language.

In theory, no matter which authoring tool is used, it will produce Web pages. However, the person responsible for stitching together the work of many authors will soon see how different the code can be. This job will be much easier if the school or district designates specific tools to use. At a minimum, provide some guidelines and limitations on what the school or district will support.

Graphics and Compression Tools

Like Web authoring tools, many graphics tools are available on the market. Although dictating the tools used may not be necessary, designating the graphics file type and size is reasonable. Graphics tools create and manipulate images; compression tools reduce the file sizes of the graphics. Consider providing a list of graphics and compression tools from which authors may choose.

Site Management, Maintenance, and Statistical Tools

Many authoring tools now come with at least some basic site management and maintenance tools built into them. These include syntax checkers that ensure the code reads properly in the browser, link checkers that make sure all the links are connected properly within the site and out to the Web, and spell checkers that check the text while skipping the code. Some report how long the pages will take to download at different connection speeds, how different browsers display the pages, whether the pages are accessible to those with disabilities, and if the graphics need better compression. These are all valuable features that may be present in the authoring tools being used. If they are not in the authoring tool of choice, some of these services are available as downloads or by subscription via the Web.

Statistical records are another site maintenance capability that should not be overlooked. Hit counters are sometimes used to show how many "hits" a page has received. A log analysis

WEB SITE STATISTICS

Analyze Your Web Site Traffic
<http://www.builder.com/Servers/Traffic/>
This article provides information and examples for numerous statistical analysis tools for use on Web sites.

Tracking Tutorial
<http://hotwired.lycos.com/webmonkey/e-business/tracking/tutorials/tutorial2.html>
This is a comprehensive and easy-to-understand tutorial about using Web site statistics.

program also tracks, but with much greater authority, exactly how many visitors come to the site and can provide a great deal of other statistical information that is useful in maintaining the site. Some of the information that statistics can show includes the following:

1. How many times the site has been visited
2. Who has visited the site
3. How visitors found the site (search tools, bookmarks, link from another site)
4. Which pages were viewed
5. Which Web browser visitors were using (*Netscape, Internet Explorer, Opera,* and so forth)
6. Which platform visitors were on (Unix, Macintosh, Windows, and so forth)
7. How long visitors stayed on a given page
8. Daily comparisons of the statistics

Statistics can provide the Web administrator or coordinator with valuable information on which sections of the site should be updated most frequently or expanded, which sections should be checked for navigation problems, which pages might be candidates for removal, and which browsers or platforms need consideration during construction. Statistics can also reveal which sites link to the school or district site and which search engines have not indexed the site well. These tools are usually located at the server level, so schools need to check with whoever is providing server space to see whether there is access to any statistics or log analysis programs.

UNDERSTANDING SPACE ALLOCATIONS

No matter on which server the site resides, the storage space available is always a specific amount. In some cases, the amount of space may be small, and schools must buy additional space if needed. Effectively using the space allocated is not only good practice but also essential to the function of the site.

Every page created has a specific file size. Every graphic, video clip, audio clip, or other multimedia file takes up additional space. A database, if present, takes another bite out of the allocation. How much schools are able to accomplish with their site sometimes depends entirely on how much space is available. Check with the server administrator to find out how much space the school has been given, then pay attention to how it gets used. Some simple ways to make good use of the space allocation include the following:

1. Reuse the same graphics on multiple pages.

2 Keep common graphics in one folder and link to them.

3 Consider whether graphics can be shared with another school by storing common files together and linking to them instead of creating copies for every school or class.

4 Apply good compression techniques to graphics to keep the file size small.

5 Do not store files that are not in use on the server.

6 Place a restriction on the file size of the graphics authors can use.

7 Create multimedia with tools that optimize files for the Web.

8 Develop retention periods that dictate how long staff and student work will stay posted, and whether it will be moved to a local archive or discarded.

9 Clean up the pages after working with an authoring tool by removing extraneous code.

10 Periodically check the space left on the server.

By knowing how much space is available, schools can judge how much they can do with the site. To find out how much space is needed, add the sizes of all files that will be loaded and compare the total to the space available. As authors work, keep an eye on the size of the files they create (especially important with multimedia files) and make sure enough space is available to handle what they develop.

▶ ORGANIZING AND NAMING FILES AND FOLDERS

The files and folders used to create the Web site require even more attention to organization than do personal files. The structure created on the server dictates how the URL will appear in a Web browser and how easy it is to maintain the site later. The length of the URL is directly related to whether the site was developed using a deep hierarchy or a flat hierarchy. (**See Chapter 9**, *What Makes a Well-Designed Educational Web Site?*, for an explanation and view of site hierarchies.) The deeper the hierarchy is, the longer the URL on the pages becomes.

Web sites tend to grow easily, and good planning at the outset will ensure that the school can accommodate the growth and easily cull when necessary. Where a page should be located on the site is obvious simply by viewing the folder structure. Grouping files that are of similar content or purpose and keeping them in a clearly named folder can help achieve this.

It is always a good idea to have a folder that contains all the images that are common throughout the site. This is where common graphics for the school can be kept, such as logos, banners, navigation buttons, divider bars, or any other images that are used on a number of pages on the site. Graphics that are used only for a special project or class page can be kept in the same folder with that page or project. In some cases, there will be a number of image folders in the structure, but they will be specific to the folder in which they reside. This method helps when culling pages from the site. If a folder for a project is removed, any graphics that are associated only with that project will also be removed, but graphics used by multiple pages will not get deleted by accident. This maintenance technique works only if school and district Web authors are aware of the structure and how to best use it.

When naming files and folders, the cardinal rule of Web publishing is that file or folder names must never include spaces or special characters. Desktop computers are liberal when allowing us to name files; the Web is not as generous in what it will process. Many servers

> **QUICK TIP**
>
> Some systems will process file and folder names with spaces in them by adding 20% in the URL wherever there is a space. However, not all systems around the world will do this. If the pages are for the Internet, do not use spaces in the file or folder names.

will not process long file names or those with spaces in the names, and when that happens, the URL breaks. Although many authoring tools are compensating by adding special characters to the file names that the servers can process, the URL becomes very difficult to read or share in these formats. A number of characters are reserved for special uses, so they should not be used. Some servers are also case sensitive. To ensure the Web site will not have problems, use these best practices when naming files and folders:

    1 Use short file and folder names.

    2 Name files using the 8.3 convention (maximum 8 characters, a dot, then 3 characters, such as .htm, .gif or .jpg).

    3 Do not use spaces in file or folder names.

    4 Do not use any of the following special characters: < > | * ? / \ " : ;

    5 Use only lower case letters.

Some servers require that specific names be applied to certain types of files. For instance, the home page may need to be named either "index" or "default" and will work only with .htm or .html as an extension. In some cases, only one name will work. The last thing a school wants to find out after creating its site is that every link to the home page has to be changed. Check with those responsible for the server to find out whether special naming conventions are required. **See** *File Name Work Sheet* in **Appendix 1**.

▶ SERVING UP PAGES FAST!

The processing speed of the server and the amount of bandwidth available will play a role in whether schools decide to include multimedia on their Web site, and if so, how much. Multimedia files could include the following:

    1 Audio clips

    2 Video clips

    3 PowerPoint or Hyperstudio presentations

Multimedia can be demanding on the server and can consume a lot of bandwidth because the file sizes are much larger than those of simple HTML files. Some multimedia tools are appearing on the market boasting small bandwidth consumption, but their consumption is still high compared to ordinary Web pages. A school or district that wants to create rich multimedia content will need to have powerful servers and plenty of bandwidth.

On the other end of the connection are visitors to the site. The school or district must consider whether the connection speeds of the visitors are fast enough to view what the school or district is serving up. Due to the download time required, visitors on dial-up connections can run into difficulty viewing large multimedia files. However, speed may not be an issue for multimedia pages or projects intended for delivery across the school or district Intranet. Decisions regarding how much multimedia the school or district will permit on the site depend largely on the target audience for the material.

LOADING RESTRICTIONS

Authors and Web team coordinators need to know exactly how to upload their pages. Do they send them to someone for uploading, or do they upload their own pages? If they upload their own pages, how do they access the server?

Schools that use a district server or host their site with an Internet Service Provider need accurate connection information. This includes a host name, a user name, and a password to access their folders on the server. If the site is uploaded using File Transfer Protocol (FTP) or by means of an authoring tool, schools need to know if special settings are required in the software they use. If schools can upload pages across an internal network (as is sometimes the case when multiple schools in a district load to a common Web server), those with authorization to load need instructions. Schools should also find out whether pages can be uploaded from home or only through the school network. These are all questions that need to be addressed ahead of time to ensure that those who have permission to load can do it when the time comes.

Clarify the types of files authors are permitted to load. If there are restrictions as to what can be loaded, schools need to be able to contact someone who works with the server and can oversee any special requests.

Uploading Web pages to the server is so simple that it is easy to forget the seriousness of the process. Many programs and scripts that can be loaded to a Web server can jeopardize the security of the server and its network. Executable files should not be loaded until the server administrator has authorized them. Any files that the Web coordinators do not recognize should not be loaded until the coordinators know what the files are and what they do. This is especially true when dealing with student folders and files. **Do not load files unless the identity and purpose is known.** Computer-savvy students will often give a reasonable explanation—but inaccurate description—of what the files are and why they are required. The safest method of dealing with these situations is to test all executable files on a secure machine. If this is not available at the school, contact the district technology department for assistance. This is another reason for restricting loading privileges to one or two staff members per school. Those two will soon begin to recognize the types of files that are high risk and what to do about them.

Many scripts are safe, however, and most Web pages today are using scripts in some way. The server administrator may have a collection of scripts that provide the school or district with the most common functions needed, including form handling, hit counters, online quizzes, and database connectivity. If scripts are available for school and district authors, the authors should be informed of what they are, where to find them, and how to make use of them.

➤ LINKING, MOVING, AND REMOVING PAGES

Inevitably, pages will be linked within a site and even among different sites on the server. Schools and districts can define for their authors how these links should be formed in order to improve performance and lessen maintenance. Links to pages on the Internet are made using absolute path names. Pages that are located within the same server should not be linked using this method—they should be linked with relative paths. An absolute path starts with http://, file:///, or a slash. A relative path name is the actual file name of the Web page, e.g., "why.html," "why/bogus.html," or ". . . /why/bogus.html."

There are a number of reasons to use relative paths for linking within the site. Linking pages on the same server using relative paths rather than absolute paths can help the pages load faster into visitors' Web browsers. Each time a full path name is used, a DNS server on the Internet must resolve the URL before sending the request to the correct location. When a relative path name is used, the Web browser looks for the page on the server it is already connected to instead of sending a request out through the Internet to find the address.

The use of relative paths also helps with the construction and maintenance of the site. Relative paths allow schools to keep a fully functional, working copy of the site on a local workstation so that schools are not working directly on the live version. As authors add and modify pages on the site, changes can be checked locally and uploaded to the server without modifying any path names. If absolute links are used, difficulties can occur with the pages once they are uploaded—this is especially true when using an authoring tool, as they will sometimes define links relative to the hard drive. **If absolute links are used between pages on the hard drive, the links will no longer work as soon as the pages are uploaded to the server.** When using an authoring tool, always check the settings to ensure that the relative paths being constructed are not those to the local computer.

As the site grows, schools and districts will find that pages or sections should be removed due to age or space restrictions. Create a plan that accommodates the removal or relocation of pages. Check pages slated for removal or relocation to see whether any other pages on the site are linked to them. Once all references to the pages have been removed, the page itself can be removed. If anyone has bookmarked the page, or if any other sites on the Web have made a link to the page, any attempt to access the page will invoke a 404 error message in the visitor's browser.

To assist those who feel that the school or district Web pages are worthy of collecting (either by linking or bookmarking the pages), many servers permit authors to create a customized 404 page that will direct users to another area of the site. This keeps visitors on the site and helps make their experience on the Web less frustrating. If the page has been relocated, visitors can find the new location. If the page has been removed, visitors can contact the owner for information. A nice by-product of custom 404 error message pages is that they will appear whenever visitors don't receive a page they have requested from your site, including the times they have typed in the address incorrectly. Check with the server administrator to see whether the school or district has the ability to create customized 404 messages for the site.

In cases where creating a customized 404 message is not possible, consider creating a referencing page when removing or relocating pages. The referencing page carries the file name of the page being removed or relocated. If the original page has been removed, the reference page states that and provides opportunity for visitors to contact the owner. If the page has been relocated, the reference page provides the new location and can be designed to automatically take visitors there after a specified time limit. Reference pages can be left in place from six months to a year and then removed completely.

⮞ PUTTING THE HOUSE IN ORDER

Clarifying and understanding the technical environment the school or district has to work with provides essential details that influence the planning, creation, and maintenance of a school or district Web site. Having this information in advance can save time, effort, and repair work for Web authors and administrators. **See** *Technical Considerations & Constraints Check Sheet* in **Appendix 1**. Many of the technical specifications required become part of the school or district publishing guidelines and policies that direct the work of all school Web authors. Taking the time to "put the technical house in order" will ensure a stable, functional, long-term school Web site.

Making It Real:
From Goals to Content

A mighty maze! but not without a plan.

—Alexander Pope

▶ MAKING A PLAN

The Web planning team has a vision, knows about types of Web pages, and is aware of policies, guidelines, copyright, support, and technical resources. The team is ready to translate the vision statement into a plan. The process involves a host of decisions. Some decisions lead to setting goals and objectives, while other decisions are made in response to goals and objectives. A formal goal-setting process is recommended. Goals, objectives, and decisions should reflect the research and input (surveys, focus groups, or discussion groups) gathered during the process of creating a vision.

Goals are general statements about desired outcomes. Use goals to address topics such as the types of pages or elements to place on a Web site. For example, a goal might be to place only original artwork on a Web site. Keep the vision statement at the forefront when developing and maintaining goals. Goals should not be static. Review, update, and revise them regularly.

Goals are traditionally grouped into three categories:

1 LONG-TERM GOALS: One to two years is recommended in Web planning. Five years is a common time length for long-term goals but is not appropriate in Web planning because of the pace of the Web.

2 MEDIUM-RANGE GOALS: Six to nine months is a good range for medium-range goals when doing Web planning.

3 **SHORT-TERM GOALS:** Six months or less is the time frame in which Web publishing goals should be accomplished.

Objectives follow goals. Objectives are plans that take goals from concepts to realities. Use objectives to manage activities, such as researching and ordering Web authoring software, or for organizing and dividing content for inclusion on a Web page. When writing objectives, make sure they are relevant, realistic, specific, and measurable. They should also have a deadline.

See these tools in **Appendix 1** that support the Web decision-making and goal-setting processes: *Web Team Decision-Planning Sheet: Questions to Consider When Making Recommendations and Setting Goals*, *Web Site Goals Worksheet*, and *Web Site Objectives Worksheet*. These tools can be used in more than one way, depending on the needs of the team. One way to use the *Web Team Decision-Planning Sheet* is to answer questions in advance to prepare for informed goal setting. Finding the information or making decisions about how to answer the questions on the *Web Team Decision-Planning Sheet* can be used to determine building or district-level Web planning goals. Use the *Web Site Goals Worksheet* for recording goals, assigning responsibilities, and targeting completion dates. The *Web Site Objectives Worksheet* is a tool for creating an action plan, assigning responsibilities, and checking progress.

Once goals and objectives are set, develop a time line using the information from the *Goals* and *Objectives* worksheets. If a number of people are responsible for meeting goals and objectives, record their names on the time line. The time line provides an overview of the whole project by showing at a glance who is responsible for what and when it is due.

COLLECTING AND CREATING CONTENT

A vision statement and goals are in place. Decisions are ready to guide the kind of Web pages and type of site to be created. It is time to work on gathering content. For *informational* pages, immediately begin to collect the facts to be shared on the site. Obtain any necessary permissions to include staff names and contact information. When creating *curricular* pages, begin work on original content. Begin deciding how to structure online lessons. Additional research may be needed before fact pages are written. Search for and save possible links. Use clearly defined standards for selecting links. Like other content, links should be compatible with the vision statement. The *Evaluating Web Sites for Linking* form in **Appendix 1** is a tool for evaluating possible online links. If the site will *showcase* student work, prepare by researching the district's Web publishing policies and guidelines. Make copies of and file the proper release forms.

Pages should be no longer than three to five computer screens. While collecting content, give some thought as to how the information might be logically divided into Web pages. Prepare to make recommendations to the site designer on the organization of materials on the Web site.

In addition to developing content, begin looking for or creating images for the Web site. Ensure that all types of content comply with copyright laws before posting them to the Internet. Check contents against the *Copyright Check Sheet* (**Appendix 1**). While content is being collected and created, Web creators can begin work on the Web site's design.

What Makes a Well-Designed Educational Web Site?

Things should be made as simple as possible, but not any simpler.

—Albert Einstein

➤ BASIC BEGINNINGS . . . BEGINNING AT THE END

What is "good" Web design? The words "Web design" often bring to mind the idea of planning a site to be visually attractive. Some people also associate it with making a plan based on the site's intended function. In educational Web design, both function and appearance are crucial considerations in the creation of a "well-designed" Web site. Good Web site design means appealing, attractive, and usable Web pages that have a unified and distinctive look throughout the Web site. (**See** *Design Check Sheet* in **Appendix 1**.)

What are the specifics of a good Web design? When people are on any page of a site, the page is recognizable as part of that site. The look of the Web page does not interfere with its use. Users do not find themselves "marooned" on pages of a Web site with no way to return to the home page. Moving around the Web site is simple. Links are consistently placed and have meaningful names. Pages load quickly and are readable. Graphics, patterns, and colors are used judiciously. Users know who is responsible for the content of the page and the age of the information.

When beginning to design a Web site, look at the vision statement. It will help answer questions that can impact the design decisions. Design questions should start with "Who is expected to use the Web site?" Is it to be used by students, teachers, the community, or other educators? What are the needs of the intended users? Does the targeted audience consist of emerging or advanced readers? Are they novices or experienced Web users? How the Web site is to be used and what it is intended to accomplish are also important considerations. Will it be used independently or in instructional situations?

 RESOURCE BOX

WEB EVALUATION

Classroom Connect's Connected Teacher—Best of the Web
<http://connectedteacher.classroom.com/library/bestofweb.asp>
Visit educational Web sites that exemplify specific aspects of Web design.

Cooke, Alison. *Authoritative Guide to Evaluating Information on the Internet.*
Neal-Schuman, 1999. Cooke provides an in-depth look at evaluating Internet resources and includes helpful checklists.

Dodge, Bernie. *A Draft Rubric for Evaluating WebQuests*
<http://edweb.sdsu.edu/webquest/webquestrubric.html>
While content is the primary focus of this evaluation form, some attention is given to design elements.

ED's Oasis Evaluation Guidelines: Educator Version
<http://www.classroom.com/edsoasis/2guide3.html>
Use this interactive Web page to evaluate educational Web sites with an online form.

EETAP. Evaluating the Content of Web Sites: Guidelines for Educators
<http://www-comdev.ag.ohio-state.edu/eetap/pdf/evalwebsites.pdf>
AND
EETAP. Evaluating the Structure of Web Sites: Guidelines for Educators
<http://www-comdev.ag.ohio-state.edu/eetap/pdf/evalstruc.pdf>
The evaluation process and evaluation points are discussed in depth in these two authoritative resources. Adobe Acrobat Reader is needed to download these documents.

EETAP. Everything You Always Wanted to Know About the Web, but Didn't Know Who to Ask
<http://www-comdev.ag.ohio-state.edu/eetap/pdf/webbroch.pdf>
This brochure provides a great overview of the Web site evaluation process. Adobe Acrobat Reader is needed to download this document.

Elkordy, Angela. Evaluating Web-based Resources: A Practical Perspective
<http://www.thelearningsite.net/cyberlibrarian/elibraries/eval.html>
This Web site includes extensive lists of evaluation points.

McLachlan, Karen. WWW CyberGuide Ratings for Content Evaluation
<http://www.cyberbee.com/guide1.html>
This evaluation form asks questions of relevance to educators.

McLachlan, Karen. WWW CyberGuide Ratings for Web Site Design
<http://www.cyberbee.com/guide2.html>
McLachlan has created a simple form that can be used to evaluate Web sites in general.

Schrock, Kathy. Critical Evaluation Survey: Virtual Tours
<http://school.discovery.com/schrockguide/evaltour.html>
Specifically intended for the evaluation of virtual tours, this form consists of a list of questions and a place for comments.

Schrock, Kathy. Kathy Schrock's Guide for Educators—Critical Evaluation Surveys
<http://school.discovery.com/schrockguide/eval.html>
Kathy Schrock's site has one of the best known and most respected evaluation resources for educators on the Internet. This evaluation resource has links to a wide range of evaluation forms, articles, and related resources.

Before designing a site, take some time to look at forms that are used to evaluate Web sites. (**See** the **Web Evaluation Resource Box**.) Although evaluation forms are intended to be used on existing sites, they can provide excellent insights into Web design. They can help Web designers identify desirable and undesirable Web elements before they make design decisions that might ultimately be design mistakes.

The exploration of existing educational Web sites can also give insights into what does and does not work. Take time to "go shopping" for ideas. (Use the resources in the **Education Online Resource Box** to locate educational Web sites.) Look for pages that do not overwhelm the user with graphics, but that use a few graphics effectively or strikingly. Check out the layouts of pages. Look at how links to other parts of the Web site are placed on the page. Watch for pages that are easy to read and think about what makes them easy to read. If possible, print examples of these "well done" sites and start example folders for the different aspects of the pages being planned. While shopping for general ideas, remember it is not ethical or legal to copy any site. This is just a "shopping trip" for design ideas.

Once the designer has a basic feel for what he or she wants to accomplish and a general idea of how to go about it, it is time to plan the specific steps that will bring about the desired results.

 RESOURCE BOX

EDUCATION ONLINE

Benson, Allen C. and Linda M. Fodemski. *Connecting Kids and the Internet: A Handbook for Librarians, Teachers, and Parents Second Edition.* Neal-Schuman, 1999, 395 pp. This handbook is a multidimensional Internet resource that includes information about highly recommended sites.

Bertland, Linda. *School Libraries on the Web: A Directory*
<http://www.sldirectory.com/index.html>
Bertland provides well-organized access to school library Web sites from around the world.

Education World's Cool Schools
<http://www.educationworld.com/cool_school/index.shtml>
Look through a collection of notable school Web sites.

Logan, Debra Kay. *Taft Library Media Center Teacher Resource Links*
<http://www.infotaft.marioncity.k12.oh.us/resour.html>
Many of the Web sites listed in the *Education Links* portion of this page feature recommended educational Web sites for educators. These sites link to the best of the best on the Web.

Milbury, Peter. *Peter Milbury's Network of School Librarian Web Pages*
<http://www.school-libraries.net/>
This site links to a host of school, library, organization, and personal Web pages created by school librarians.

Miller, Elizabeth. *The Internet Resource Directory for K–12 Teachers and Librarians: 2000/2001 Edition.* Libraries Unlimited, 2000, 462 pp.
Miller's directory is a leading source.

University of Minnesota. *Web66: A K–12 World Wide Web Project*
<http://web66.coled.umn.edu/>
Probably the best known directory of school Web sites, Web66 lists school Web sites by countries and regions.

This book divides those steps into three groups of design decisions: access, format, and content. Although whole books are written on the subject of Web design, this chapter is intended to provide an overview and to highlight points that can be used to create excellent educational Web sites.

STEP ONE: ASSURING ACCESS

In Chapter 4, *Blueprints for a Firm Foundation: Publishing Guidelines and Policies,* "accessibility" refers to making a Web site accessible to individuals with disabilities who are using adaptive equipment or to individuals using older equipment or browsers. Access can also relate to how a site is structured. Site structure looks at how the pages are connected to one another. Those connections determine how users move around a Web site. It is also necessary to make decisions about the navigation tools that surfers will use to move from page to page in a site. The layout of individual pages will also impact access to the information being shared. Each of these elements will contribute to the usability of a Web site.

Accessibility

Because some individuals use adaptive equipment, older computers, low speed Internet connections, or older browsers, it is important to know the Web site's intended audience and what types of equipment they may be using. It is necessary to accommodate special needs, and a few simple adjustments can make a Web site more accessible. Actually, some of the accessibility adjustments make good design sense even if the targeted audience does not need the adjustments. Designing for accessibility can result in cleaner-looking sites with faster download times.

Graphics are a good place to start making a site accessible. Avoid the use of extensive graphics. Be sure to include and use attributes. ALT (descriptive text that appears as an *alternative* to a graphic image) attributes are the little lines of text that pop up when a surfer puts a cursor over a Web page image. If some of the intended users are using text readers, ALT attributes allow users who are visually impaired to "read the pictures." If large graphics are necessary, use thumbnails.

Applets are the scrolling text that can be found on Web sites. Alternative code (descriptive text) is needed for Applets to be "read" by some forms of assistive technologies.

Although image maps are attractive, they are large graphics and can cause problems for individuals with adaptive equipment or less powerful connections or browsers. Image maps can also be confusing to less experienced users. Make a site more accessible by including alternatives to image maps. Text navigation links should be included along with image maps. Another option is to provide users the option of using alternative "text only" pages.

Tables can cause accessibility problems. Tables are often used to position information and page elements on a Web site. Because tables were originally created to contain data, using them to structure the look of a page can make pages unreadable for individuals using adaptive equipment. Fortunately, newer adaptive equipment handles tables better than earlier equipment. Cascading Style Sheets (CSS) are an alternative to tables for creating page layouts. **(Warning: CSS are not always completely supported by browsers, such as *Netscape* and *Internet Explorer*.)** If using tables is necessary, do some labeling. Start by giving a table a title. Write descriptive notes for use in **caption elements** to describe the contents of a table. Caption elements are text-based descriptive notes that give information about a table for people using adaptive equipment. A table summary is another text-based tool for providing descriptions. Use table **summary attributes** to explain the structure and purpose of a table.

FAST FACT

Thumbnails are smaller, lower-resolution versions of an image. See the Image section of this chapter for more information about thumbnails.

FAST FACT

Some Web authoring tools give the Web author the option of using Cascading Style Sheets (CSS).

CSS can be used to specify a consistent look for a Web site. With CSS, the layout, colors, and other basic details of a site's pages are set once and then automatically appear throughout the pages of a Web site. Aspects of CSS are incompatible with some Web browsers, and the use of CSS can cause usability problems.

Tables are not the only page elements that can cause difficulties with accessibility. Frames and forms can also block accessibility. Adaptive equipment does not open all the layers of a framed page. If a Web site has frames, also provide frame-free access. If forms are to be placed on a Web site, include descriptive text for input areas. Also, label controls. If the form lists options, they should be grouped logically to simplify use.

Avoid plug-ins if accessibility is a concern. A plug-in is special software that needs to be downloaded to hear sounds or movies on Web sites. If streaming audio or video is included on a Web site, caption it to make it accessible. Captioning is time-consuming and can be a copyright problem because it is essentially an adaptation. PDF files have been inaccessible to individuals using text readers and other adaptive equipment. PDF stands for Portable Document Format. Software such as *Adobe Acrobat Reader* can open and read PDF files on the Web. A simple explanation of a PDF file is that it is a picture of text. New technology makes PDF files accessible.

JavaScript can also interfere with accessibility. JavaScript is a form of coding that can be used in many ways on a Web site. For example, some of its uses include making words move across Web pages, creating forms, and making drop-down menus. Unfortunately, while JavaScript can make a site more interactive and usable, it can also interfere with the use of assistive technologies such as text readers. Users with older Web browsers may not be able to use a Web site if the pages have JavaScript. Some people might think that the solution to this problem is to update browsers, but sometimes older computers cannot handle newer versions of browsers. Mouse rollovers are a use of JavaScript that interferes with accessibility. Examples of mouse rollovers are a Web page item changing color or a text box popping up as a mouse is being moved over a Web page. If the information conveyed by the rollovers is not available in alternative ways, the information is inaccessible to some users.

Does this mean that every site has to be designed to be accessible for every kind of user and computer? That

QUICK TIP

ALT attributes are often referred to as ALT tags.

would be virtually impossible. Should Web designers design just for the specific set of computers and browsers in their schools? Focusing on a particular set of computers or one type of browser will ultimately limit the usefulness of a Web site. Designing with a particular set of computers or browser could be especially limiting if a school has fabulously fast connections and powerful computers, and sites are designed accordingly. Students, teachers, and the community may not be able to use the Web site on their computers at home. Other schools may not be able to utilize the resources provided. Again, what to do? This is a difficult question. There are many different computer systems, browsers, and so forth. It is important to target primary and secondary audiences and to design with their needs in mind. Once a site has been created, test it by opening the Web pages on a variety of computers and browsers. Make certain the site can be opened with both *Netscape Communicator* and *Internet Explorer*. Try opening the site with older and newer versions of those programs. Look at the Web site on different size monitors. Change the monitor settings and view it in black and white. Change the screen resolution and check the results. Know that there is a chance that someone somewhere will not be able to use the site. Try to make sure that the site is accessible to the targeted primary and secondary users.

To learn more about making a site accessible, check out the Web sites listed in the **Accessibility Resource Box** on page 93.

Site Structure

Now it is time to map out the Web site. A Web site's structure determines how the user moves around the Web site. The nature of the site's content is a primary consideration when selecting a site's structure. After thinking about the kind of information being shared on the site, look at different ways the content can be divided, grouped, and organized. With that information in mind, now look at the different ways a Web site can be structured.

Web sites begin with an opening page called the "home page." It is important to remember that every page in a Web site should link to the home page. Beyond that home page, additional pages can be connected in a variety of ways. Of the three most common kinds of site structures, the most frequently found is **hierarchical (Figure 9-1)**. In a hierarchical structure, the user starts at the top or the home page and moves "down" through the

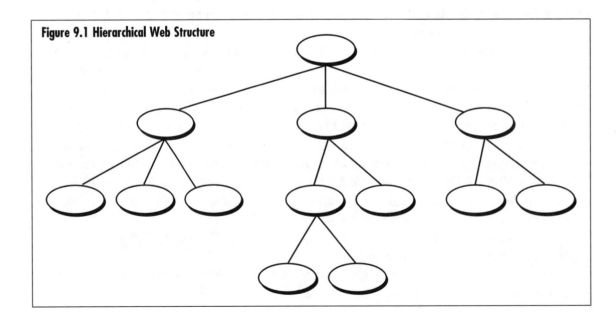

Figure 9.1 Hierarchical Web Structure

ACCESSIBILITY

About.Com: Accessibility and the Web
<http://html.miningco.com/compute/html/cs/accessibility/index.htm>
Webmaster Jennifer Kyrnin has assembled a wide assortment of resources and tools related to Web accessibility.

Accessible Web Page Design
<http://www.eskimo.com/~jlubin/disabled/web-desi.html>
Here are links to accessibility resources.

Bobby
<http://www.cast.org/bobby/>
Use Bobby to check pages for accessibility barriers. Bobby identifies and explains accessibility problems. Sites passing the check can put the Bobby icon on their site.

Federal IT Accessibility Initiative
<http://www.section508.gov/>
Under Section 508 of the Rehabilitation Act, U.S. federal agencies' information technologies are required to be accessible. This Web site was created to assist with the process of making technologies accessible.

Paciello, Michael. *Web Accessibility for People with Disabilities*. CMP Books, 2000.
Paciello covers legal issues related to Web accessibility and provides detailed information on how to make Web sites accessible.

Paciello, Michael. WebABLE
<http://www.webable.com/>
A wide assortment of accessibility resource links and information can be found on this site.

Usability.gov
<http://usability.gov/>
This resource provides assistance with designing accessible Web sites.

W3C Web Accessibility Initiative
<http://www.w3.org/WAI/>
AND
W3C Web Content Accessibility Guidelines 1.0
http://www.w3.org/TR/WAI-WEBCONTENT/
Utilize both the W3C Web site and Guidelines page for extensive information about Internet accessibility.

Wave 2.01
<http://www.temple.edu/inst_disabilities/piat/wave/>
Wave is an online tool for checking Web site accessibility. Wave provides a detailed accessibility analysis of Web sites and explains results.

Figure 9.2 Web or Interconnected Structure

site layer by layer. It is similar to a family tree or the structure of a corporate organizational chart.

The type of Web structure that best utilizes the nature of the Internet is the Web or interconnected structure (**Figure 9.2**). In sites planned with a Web-type structure, every page is connected to all of the other pages. Users can move easily throughout the Web site. If possible, this is the type of structure that should be the goal when a site is designed.

Linear is the third common type of Web structure (**Figure 9.3**). It is frequently used for presentations and tutorials. It can be used to take a user through a step-by-step process. Early versions of *PowerPoint* presentations are examples of linear structure. When planning a linear arrangement, give users some navigational options—this is important. One of the things that people like the most about the Internet is feeling in control by getting to make choices about where to go next. At the very least, provide users with a chance to move home, backward, or forward.

Sometimes Web sites combine aspects of two or more of the three structures (**Figure 9.4**). A site with a predominantly Web structure could have a section with a linear tutorial. A linear tutorial could have a page with a hierarchical structure that gives users the option of dropping

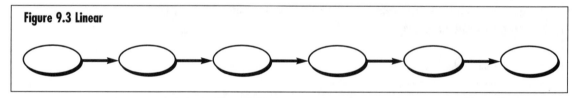
Figure 9.3 Linear

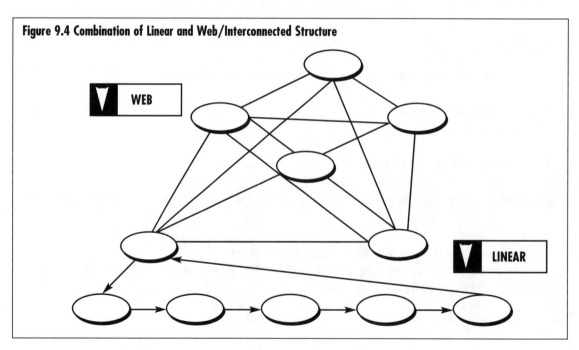
Figure 9.4 Combination of Linear and Web/Interconnected Structure

WEB

LINEAR

down through layers of pages to further explore the topic before moving on to the tutorial's next topic. An online tutorial could be designed to be used in a linear fashion and still give the user opportunities to select and move to specific pages in the tutorial. This would combine the step-by-step presentation of information with Web structure access.

Storyboarding may help with the selection of a site arrangement. Try putting the names of a site's Web pages on index cards or sticky notes and moving them into different arrangements. If preferred, graphic-organizing software, such as *Inspiration,* can be used to map out a site. For some people, a simple outline is all that is needed to "see" the structure of a Web site. Try a variety of arrangements. During this process, remember that the Web site needs to be planned to allow for future growth and the possibilities of other uses. Plan and design for flexibility.

Navigation

After determining the arrangement and relationships of pages, think about how people will make connections to move from page to page. One of the first criteria used to evaluate a site is how easy it is for users to move around the site. Make moving around a Web site as easy as possible. There are a handful of simple guidelines that make a Web site easy to navigate.

A cardinal rule is to make certain that every page links to the home page. Avoid stranding users on orphan pages. Orphan pages do not have any links back to their original site. They can be particularly frustrating if there is no way to identify the source of the page. If possible, interconnect all pages.

Navigation menus should have a consistent look and should be found at consistent locations on Web pages. Aim for "transparent navigation"—so obvious that it's transparent. Visitors to a site should never think, "How do I get to . . ." for long enough to realize that they are even thinking. Navigation menus are frequently found at the top, along the side, or at the bottoms of Web pages. Ideally, they should be highly visible on the opening or top screen of every Web page. At the least, they should be visible in the opening screen of a site's home page. If using an image map for the menu, it is critical to also provide text versions of the links. Include directions so that Internet newbies understand how to use the image map.

The names of navigation links are usually page or site names. It is important that those names reflect the page's content. Link names should be meaningful and easy to understand at a glance. Users should be able to locate the desired content on a Web site with one click and not by trial and error. If a page is not yet completed, do not create a link to it, because "under

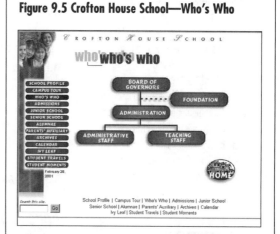

Figure 9.5 Crofton House School—Who's Who

\<http://www.croftonhouse.bc.ca/croftonhouse/whowho.htm\>

Visitors to this site will find it easy to navigate due to the consistent menus and clear, logical presentation of content. *Marcelle Adam/Pinnacles & Prisms, Web Site Administrator, Crofton House School, Vancouver, British Columbia, Canada*

Figure 9.6 A WebQuest About Evaluating Web Sites

A WebQuest About Evaluating Web Sites

http://mciu.org/~spjvweb/evalwebstu.html

For 9-12 Graders

Joyce Valenza

Introduction | Task | Resources | Process | Evaluation | Conclusion

Introduction

If you are like most students, you are relying heavily on resources from the Web for your research. Not all Web resources are created equal. If fact, there are great variations in the quality of the resources you access. The rule of thumb is "when in doubt, doubt." When you carefully select your resources, when you understand their strengths and limits, you create better products.

The Task

You will be working in groups of four to evaluate a group of Web pages on the topic of tobacco and smoking, or cloning or another topic of your teacher's choice. Each of you will be examining sites from a different perspective. You will be ranking the sites and comparing your rankings with the rest of the class.

`<http://mciu.org/~spjvweb/evalwebstu.html>`
Students can easily move to the various parts of this WebQuest Web page using the page menu. Each section of the page has a clear, meaningful title, making navigation easy. *Joyce Valenza, Springfield Township High School, Erdenheim, Pennsylvania*

construction" pages are considered bad Web design.

Navigation is not just limited to helping users move from page to page. Be sure to provide ways for users to easily move around on long pages. Place page menus at the top of pages. Give portions of the page appropriate, clear names. Include "Back to the top" links at regular intervals in longer pages.

Another rule of thumb is to avoid push pages. Push pages move users automatically to other pages, not giving the surfer any choices. These kinds of pages usually irritate users who like being in control of their Internet use. The one time that these pages are considered acceptable is when they move the user from an outdated Web address to the current address. Sometimes push pages are "splash" pages, which are usually striking pages with a logo or image and not much else. They take a long time to load and usually serve no meaningful purpose for the user. A user will appreciate a logo more if it is tasteful, fast-loading, and consistently placed in all of a Web site's pages—and not found on a splash page. Not all splash pages are meaningless; some can serve useful purposes. A splash page can be used to give visitors the option of selecting between different versions of a site. Users may be asked to make choices, such as "with frames or without frames?" or "French or English?" Push pages can also be "Flash" pages. Flash pages are often filled with what Jakob Nielson calls "gratuitous animation"—the user is forced to sit through animations (*Alertbox: Flash 99% Bad* <http://www.useit.com/alertbox/20001029.html>). Because Flash is not standard HTML, it disables some browser controls. For example, back buttons do not work. It is possible for the designer to provide a move to provide a "next page" button that allows the user to skip a Flash page, giving the user some control.

Page Layout

When users move around a site, all the pages should look as if they are a part of the same Web site. As surfers link to another page in a site, the surfers should have a good idea of what the next page will look like before it downloads. This uniformity is achieved through consistent use of backgrounds, colors, images, and arrangements or layouts on Web pages.

> **QUICK TIP**
>
> When linking to page within a site, it is better to write with relative path names instead of absolute path names. An absolute path name is the address for that Web page, e.g., http://www.infotaft.marioncity.k12.oh.us/why/bogus.html. An absolute path stars with http://, file:///, or a slash. A relative path name is the actual file name of the Web page, e.g., "why.html," "why/bogus.html," or "../why/bogus.html." When an absolute name is used, the links work only when the computer being used is online because the address is a Web address. When a relative name is used, the link will work when the computer is offline. That convention makes doing Web work on a site much easier.

> **FAST FACT**
>
> Though different from the "bookmarks" found in some browsers, the name given to a section of a Web page to accommodate navigation is "bookmark."

When beginning to lay out a page, think about the placement of these essential page elements:

1 Logo(s)

2 Headings

3 Navigation tools/menus

4 Background images

5 Content

6 Contact/responsibility information

7 Copyright information

8 Update information

9 Other

Map out the basic page design using pencil and paper, a drawing program, or a Web page editor (**Figure 9.7**). Decide the locations for the necessary elements on a basic page. Are

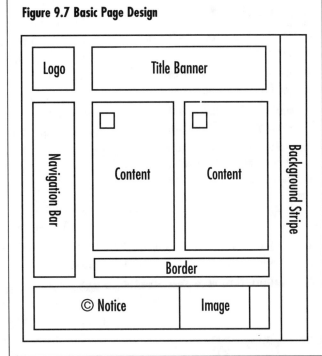

Figure 9.7 Basic Page Design

elements to be placed on the top, bottom, right, or left portion of the page? Keep in mind that white or empty space is an important part of a Web page. Users need to have spaces to rest their eyes. When completed, a basic page should have a look that is consistent, clear, simple, and uncluttered. It should highlight important information. Having a clean, simple, and consistent look does not mean that a Web site is not distinctive and striking.

Once the page layout is planned, create a template page (save as template.html or template.htm) that can be used each time work is begun on a new Web page. Each new page is then saved using "save as" under its own file name (e.g., pageone.html or pageone.htm).

When naming files, remember the 8.3 standard global naming convention discussed in Chapter 7, *Technical Considerations*. While working on a template, make certain that users will not need to scroll horizontally.

When designing a template, there are several ways to control the look of a Web page. Cascading Style Sheets can be used to designate properties for all of the Web pages that are part of a group of Web pages. They are not entirely supported by all browsers. A more common option is to use tables to position objects in cells. Tables can help with arranging and positioning the various textual and graphic elements of a Web page. When using a table as the foundation for a Web page, it is possible to better accommodate some viewing variables. A table or table cells can be structured to appear as a specific size on a monitor by setting them to be a certain number of pixels. Although this approach gives

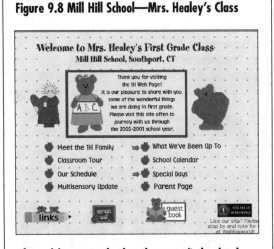

Figure 9.8 Mill Hill School—Mrs. Healey's Class

<http://www.mrshealeysclass.com/index.html>
This site appeals to students as well as to parents. It is well-designed, consistent, and easy to read and understand. This excellent classroom site informs, communicates, celebrates student work, and even raises funds with style. *Paula Healey, Mill Hill School, Southport, Connecticut*

the webmaster a great deal of control, it can cause some problems due in part to monitor settings and printer limitations. Monitors can be set for resolutions as low as 640 by 480 pixels. Higher resolutions have a large range of settings. If a table is created for a greater number of pixels than the monitor is set to view, the user will need to scroll horizontally; printers may not be able to print the complete page, and portions of the page do not print. Horizontal scrolling aggravates Web users. If using pixels to determine table size, the designer can avoid horizontal scrolling by using the lowest monitor setting size (640 by 480 pixels). When a page is laid out using a table and the lower settings for pixels, a Web site will work well on a monitor set for low resolution but will look ridiculously tiny on a high-resolution monitor.

A more flexible way to use tables to structure Web pages is to set them to specified percentages. The size of a table can be set to be 80% of the screen. The table will compact the

page to fit 80% of a low-resolution monitor or stretch it to fill 80% of a high-resolution monitor. Using percentages can be more flexible, but still problematic. Defining table size by percentages causes the computer to determine the size and shape of some Web page elements. Because graphic sizes are defined in pixels, they are not flexible. As a result, the portions of the page that are flexible may be crunched or stretched to compensate. Text may be broken in odd ways. Combining the use of pixels and percentages can sometimes bring the best results. For example, a Web designer might set the table at 80% but set certain cell sizes by pixels to make sure that text is not chopped.

In the past, having long pages that require extensive vertical scrolling was considered poor design because a high percentage of Web users did not scroll down Web pages. During the short history of the World Wide Web, that is changing. Users are becoming more sophisticated and now do know to scroll down but will do so only if the content is of interest. Still, unless content is compelling, it is wise to limit the length of a page to no longer than three to five computer screens. At those lengths, be sure to provide a page menu and "Back to the top" links to facilitate navigating on the page.

Starting with the basic template, it is important to design a home page horizontally. That means that nearly the entire home page is visible on a computer screen when the home page is opened. The navigational tools, page title, and logo should all be visible on the opening screen.

Once the structure, navigation, and layout of a Web site is determined, it is important to take a close look at the Web page elements.

▷ STEP TWO: FUNCTIONAL FORMATS

At a glance, images, colors, and text sound like the fun and artistic elements of Web design. They can be used to set a site's tone and look. They can also impact the usability and readability of a site. There are a few things to know about using images, colors, and text that can help Web workers achieve a desired look.

FAST FACT

Interlacing is another technique to cut wait time when loading images. An interlaced image downloads in layers.

As layers are added, the image becomes sharper and clearer. GIF and PNG formats can be interlaced. JPEGs can be progressive; these are a form of interlacing.

Images

Have you ever waited and waited for a page to download and then decided to stop it and try a different page? Long download times will turn off and turn away users. Great graphics, compelling content, and the best Web sites will not be seen if frustrated users hit the back button before the page finishes downloading. The total download time for a Web page should be no more than about 30 seconds.

One of the easiest ways to keep download times manageable is to use images judiciously. Graphic sizes are measured in kilobytes (KB). On a 14.4 modem, 35 KB of graphics takes about 31 seconds to download. With a 28.8 modem, 35 KB of graphics takes about 15 seconds to download. Add the sizes of graphics to be placed on a Web page. Keep the total under 30 to 35 KB. Some Web authoring tools automatically calculate the size of graphics on a Web page.

Because graphics stop or interrupt readers as they are trying to read, limiting the number of graphics will help improve download times and make the site more readable. Reusing graphics also decreases download times. Once an image has been downloaded, the computer will not have to download it over and over during an online session. When a Web page is being constructed, specify sizes for images. This technique improves download time because it enables the browser to set aside the amount of space needed for the graphic. The text portions of the page can be downloaded immediately, so the visitor can start reading without waiting for the graphic to download.

Using thumbnail images is another way to speed up download times. Thumbnails are smaller, low-resolution versions of an image. These smaller images load faster than full-size images. Use a photo-editing program to create them. Start by copying the image to produce two versions of it. One is the full-size version and the other is the thumbnail. Reduce the image dimensions by cropping and resizing the image. Cut the file size of both versions of the image by reducing them to 256 colors. Save the thumbnail image at 72 dpi (dots per inch) to further reduce its file size. Use the thumbnail image on the Web page with the related content. Make the thumbnail into a link to the full-size image, which is still the complete full-size image that has been created at a higher resolution, such as 100 or 144 dpi. Because monitors can handle only up to certain resolutions, finer resolutions do not benefit screen display. The higher-resolution image will look better if it is downloaded and printed.

In addition to keeping download times low, consider other image guidelines. Avoid busy background—they make pages difficult to read. Because graphics interfere with reading, limit the number of graphics and think carefully about where graphics are placed on the page. Large banners can cause problems such as long download times and horizontal scrolling. Keep banners small enough that they do not force users to scroll horizontally. Some types of images have been overused; they may be considered amateurish, so use them

FAST FACT

Flashing/blinking text or graphics can render a Web site inaccessible because they can trigger epileptic seizures.

GRAPHICS FORMATS FOR WEB PAGES

	NAME:	SAVE AS:	USE:
GIF	**G**raphics **I**nterchange **F**ormat	graphic.gif	GIF is the format usually used for line drawings, or for images with few or single colors. GIFs have a maximum of 256 colors. GIFs can be animated. Some colors can be made transparent in GIFs. They will work on Macs or PCs and in most browsers.
JPEG	**J**oint **P**hotographic **E**xperts **G**roup	graphic.jpg or graphic.jpeg (on a Mac)	JPEG is the format usually used for photographs, art, and other types of full color images. JPGs can have as many as 16.7 million colors. They also can be used on Macs or PCs and in most browsers.
PNG	**P**ortable **N**etwork **G**raphics	graphic.png	PNG is a format that can be used cross platform and is highly compressed (can be made smaller than GIFs). Like a JPG, a PNG can have 16.7 million colors. PNGs can also be gray scale. The PNG images do not lose date when files are saved and resaved. Interlaced PNGs form a more discernable image more quickly than GIFs or JPGs. PNG is not as well supported by browsers as JPEGs and GIFs at this time and may require plug-ins. Browser support is improving.

In the above file names, the word, "graphic" stand for a file name.

with restraint. These images include animated .gifs, image bars, scrolling text, flashing or blinking text, and counters. If a counter is needed to document use, keep it small or even hidden on the page.

Here are some image "do's." Use color images instead of black and white. When using graphics, do use ALT attributes. The webmaster embeds ALT attributes into the coding of a Web site. In addition to making a Web site more accessible, ALT attributes are helpful when an image does not download correctly. The user can see the description of the image that should have downloaded. It is a good idea to use ALT attributes for every image. Do check for acceptable use guidelines before using graphics. Do credit image creators. (**See** Chapter 5 *Copyright Issues and the Web* for more information about using copyright protected materials on a Web site.)

Color

Designing with color on the Web means doing more than just selecting attractive color combinations. Older monitors are limited to 256 colors. There are 216 colors that are common to the operating

 RESOURCE BOX

COLOR AND THE WEB

The Hexadecimal Color Learning Center
<http://www.stfrancis.edu/cid/Colors/hex.htm>
Learn about color and the Internet on this informative site.

HTML 3.0 Color Code Table
<http://www.westsound.com/westsound/Help/color.html>
See the hexadecimal colors with their codes on this chart.

Web Color Calculator
<http://labrocca.com/colorcalc/>
Here is help with selecting compatible colors.

Colormaker
<http://www.bagism.com/colormaker/>
This is a cool tool that helps the user generate safe colors and add texture to a Web site.

ColorCenter
<http://www.hidaho.com/colorcenter/>
Test colors at this site. It offers links to a variety of resources.

systems of various types of computers. If one of the 40 other colors is used, the browser selects a replacement color or "mixes" its own color. This can result in disastrous colors when the Web page is displayed. The 216 Web or browser safe colors are based on RGB (red, green, and blue) and are listed in what is called the Hexadecimal Color Chart. It is easy to tell at a glance if a color is Web/browser safe by looking at the hex value. If it is made up with a combination of 00, 33, 66, 99, CC, or FF, the color is Web/browser safe. If the color includes other values, it is not Web/browser safe. "99," "00," and "CC" are all on the list of safe values, so 9900CC is a Web/browser safe color. "55" is not on the list, so 559900 would not be a Web/browser safe color.

When planning Web pages, the designer has a number of opportunities to select colors. The designer can pick colors of backgrounds, table cells, and horizontal lines. When there were fewer experienced Web users, designers were advised to reserve blue for links. Now that Web users are generally more sophisticated, designers can safely choose the colors of new, active, and visited links. Keep the following factors in mind when making these color decisions. If selecting a gray background or text, remember that some people are color-blind; unless the background and text are highly contrasted, they may not be able to discern the text. Putting text on medium or dark backgrounds negatively impacts legibility and reading comprehension. Even light text on a dark background is difficult to read. Using dark text on a light background is both attractive and readable. Use color to draw attention to bits of text. Do not use the same colors for links and highlighting.

> **FAST FACT**
>
> The most readable combination is black text on a white or yellow background. Higher contrast between text and background results in higher readability.

> **FAST FACT**
>
> Just as there are safe colors for the Web, there are safe fonts.
>
> The fonts that a designer selects for a page may not be what surfers see. If a designer specifies a font that is not available on a user's computer, the user will probably see the page in a default font, such as Times New Roman. The safest fonts for Macs are Times, Helvetica, and Courier. Safe fonts for PCs include Times New Roman, Arial, and Courier New. Some other fonts that are commonly found in browsers are Geneva, Trebuchet, MSP Impact, Veranda, Georgia, and Comic Sans. Georgia has been found to be the best font for educational purposes.
>
> Web users can also use browser preference settings to select a font. The selected font then overrides the Web site's designated fonts.

Colors have cultural significance and affect people emotionally. Red represents luck and celebrations in China and purity in India. While black is a color for mourning in Western cultures, white is the color for mourning in Eastern cultures. Blue is a holy color in the Jewish religion; in China it is associated with immortality. In Columbia, blue is equated with soap. For an international audience, blue is considered the safest of colors. About.com's Web design expert Jean Kaiser, in *Color in Web Design* <http://webdesign.about.com/compute/webdesign/library/weekly/aa082399.htm>, has put together an excellent guide about color and culture and the effects of color.

> **FAST FACT**
>
> Logos are copyrighted. Check before putting them on a Web page.

The emotional impact of colors is well documented, and Kaiser notes cultural and symbolic concepts that are associated with various colors. Red is an excellent choice to excite people. Americans also associate red with violence, blood, and war. To project the image of stability, consider blue or gray. Blue can be equated with depression and gray with boredom.

Think about the audience and message when making decisions about appropriate colors. Color can be key

> **FAST FACT**
>
> Web usability guru Jakob Nielsen has found that the PDF format cuts Web usability between 280% and 320% compared to the usability of pages created in HTML.
>
> Nielsen's June 10, 2001 report, *Avoid PDF for On-Screen Reading* <http://www.useit.com/alertbox/20010610.html>, recommends using only PDF for pages that users are likely to print.

in achieving a "look." A site can have a fun, professional, mysterious, or some other type of look. The school or the project the page is representing may already have logos and colors associated with it. In that case, it is critical to send a consistent message. Tastefully incorporate those colors and images into the Web page.

Text

Educators may be surprised to learn that most people do not actually read the Internet. Research shows that the majority of people scan Web pages or just look at the pictures. People are less likely to read things on the Internet because reading a computer screen is harder for the eyes than reading a printed page—it's 25% slower to read a computer screen. A designer can do a number of things to minimize eye stress and to make pages more legible and readable:

FAST FACT

Arial and Comic Sans Serif are examples of sans serif fonts.

FAST FACT

Serif fonts, such as Times New Roman, increase legibility on printed pages.

1 Limit type to 25% to 30% of the Web page.

2 Aim for lines of type with between 40 to 60 characters per line. The lines of type on a page should be about the width of a book. If creating columns of text on a Web page, limit columns to 30 to 40 characters per line.

3 Keep font size between 10 and 14 points.

4 Do not center or justify a body of text. Centering and justifying reduce readability. Align text to the left.

5 Do not use all capital letters. They reduce readability and take up as much as 30% more space. As in e-mail, all capital letters is rude because it is considered shouting.

6 Use combinations of upper and lower case letters when appropriate.

7 Use the same font style or font family throughout the Web site.

8 Use a sans serif font when creating Web pages. Fonts without serifs are more clearly defined and more legible on Web pages.

9 Select fonts with well-defined ascenders (the part that rises above the main part of the letters b, d, f, h, k, l, or t) and descenders (the part that drops below the main portion of the letters g, j, p, q, or y).

10 Do not use italics.

11 Do not use white or pale colors for text or links. They are difficult to print.

12 Avoid long paragraphs.

13 Put borders around important information.

14 Take advantage of visual focal points; Web pages have two. Viewers start reading at the upper left corner of a Web page and tend to look at the area one-third of the way down the page on the right.

15 Use, but do not overuse, bold, italics, and underlining to highlight key words.

16 Make the page easy to scan by using headings, subheadings, lines, and color. Change font sizes and colors, but not frequently. Too many font sizes and colors turn Web pages into a veritable circus and

FAST FACT

Legibility and readability have different meanings.
Legibility is how easy or difficult it is to read bits of text. How easy is it to make out letters and words? **Readability** is how easy or difficult it is to read chunks or blocks of text. Is it easy or tough to read a long online article?

Both legibility and readability have implications for making a Web site accessible to possible users. Users with difficulties such as learning disabilities need sites that are legible and readable. Make every effort to optimize both legibility and readability.

decrease readability. The top headings should identify what is important about the page.

- ✒ Use bulleted or numbered lists to slow scanners and to draw attention to important information.
- ✒ Put blank lines between paragraphs instead of indenting or using tabs.
- ✒ Write captions for images.

▶ STEP THREE: CREATING CONTENT

Good design is not limited to ensuring that a Web site is accessible and the formats are functional. Web site content also has design implications. Make sure that pages are worth the download time. For the right content, users will wait a long time. Pages abound on the Web that are flashy, glitzy, and without substance. Although users may be initially attracted to these types of pages, they will not stay there. Users are looking for pages that are relevant, user-friendly, and readable. Surfers need pages that are accurate, complete, objective, clear, and current. They want pages that are unique and appealing. Web sites can be all of those things, and content is of the utmost importance. Content can take many forms. Design implications for content impact the handling of links, writing, establishing authority, and multimedia resources on Web pages.

Links

Listing links on a site is a type of content. In *Making Best Use of the Internet to Enhance Your School Library Program* (Bureau of Education and Research, 2000), Peter Milbury, webmaster of the internationally recognized *Chico High School Library Helpful Bookmarks* < http://dewey.chs.chico.k12.ca.us/ >, wrote, "The cardinal rule of Web collection development is to make certain that your goal is to always focus on the curriculum." Select links carefully. Any time an external link is placed on a Web site, the user is being sent away. Think about where the user is being sent and why. Make certain that Web visitors are sent to valuable sites that will make them want to come back to your Web site to find out what other links the site has to offer. When selecting links for the Web site, use Web evaluation criteria (**See** *Evaluating Web Sites for Linking* in **Appendix 1**). Those criteria might include

> **QUICK TIP**
>
> An alternative to sending users away from a Web site via links is to code the links in such a way that an additional browser window opens the "linked to" Web page. Be aware that this is a somewhat controversial practice that sometimes is mentioned on lists of Web design pet peeves.

> **QUICK TIP**
>
> Found a great site and want to create a link to it, but a frame of another site blocks the address of the great site? Use the "history" feature of the Web browser to uncover the address of a Web site accessed through a Web site frame.

> **QUICK TIP**
>
> When annotating your links, avoid including statistics about the site to which you are linking. If the link-to site has 550 links today, it may have 1,000 links next week. This is a maintenance nightmare.

Figure 9.9 Lawrence High School Library

<http://library.lhs.usd497.org/primarysources.htm>
Not only does this site have consistent layout and design but its fully annotated links to evaluated Web resources also give visitors a description of the site to help them decide which resources are best for their needs. *Martha Oldman, Librarian, Lawrence High School, Lawrence, Kansas*

QUICK TIP

Keep links up-to-date. Schedule regular checks for bad links. This is an activity that can be easily turned over to students with a minimum of training.

QUICK TIP

When creating links, link to the page with the desired information and not to the site's opening page. Do not expect users to "click" through layers of pages to find the needed information. The exception to this is when the "link to" site specifies that deep linking is not permitted.

QUICK TIP

It is helpful to put the address of the page in the footer with the signature and date. This makes citing the page simpler and provides an address if the page is found in the frame of another Web site.

age appropriateness, reading level, user friendliness, validity of links, authority, lack of bias, currency, accuracy, relevancy, uniqueness, and overall quality.

Once links are selected, determine how to organize them. They should be grouped by subject and alphabetized by title. Try to avoid having more than 30 links on a single page. Along with the linked page's title and URL, links should include annotations. Use annotations to give users clear and brief pictures of what they can find on the other side of the link. Tell users the highlights found on the page to which the link is being made. By including the site's URL with the annotation, a Web site that is a great online resource also becomes a useful annotated resource that can be used online or printed for reference. Avoid including the words "click here" when writing link annotations.

Writing

Writing for the Web is a bit different from other kinds of writing. Most readers scan Web pages. Few users read Web pages the way they read a book or a magazine article. Jakob Nielsen reports his and John Morkes' findings on how people view Web pages in *Alertbox: How Users Read on the Web* <http://www.useit.com/alertbox/9710a.html>: Instead of reading a Web page word-for-word, 79% of Web users always scan Web pages. Only 16% of the Web users read Web pages word-by-word. The readability of a Web site impacts its accessibility.

To increase readability, use an inverted-pyramid approach to writing. This is the type of writing typically found in newspapers and in encyclopedia articles. Put the conclusion or the most important information at the top of the page where it is most likely to be read. Write captions for graphics.

To further make Web writing easy to scan, avoid writing in paragraphs. Use short phrases or outlines. Whenever possible, limit paragraphs to one idea and to four or fewer sentences. Keep sentences simple and information brief and to the point. Use fewer words on Web pages than on printed pages. The word count of a Web page should be only 50% of the words used on a printed page when putting equivalent information on the Web page.

Authority

When creating a Web site, it is important to send the message that it is credible and reliable. Hopefully, users evaluate Web sites by looking for the same kinds of clues taught to students in evaluating Web sites.

Establish credibility by making certain that every page is signed and that it includes the name of the sponsoring organization (the school or district). List the date the page was created or the date of the most recent update. Provide a contact e-mail address on each page. Put the address of the page in the footer with the signature. Include a page somewhere on the site that has the credentials of the sites' webmaster or authors. Credit sources of information and graphics.

The bottom or footer of the page should have the following kinds of information:

Multimedia

As discussed in Chapter 7, *Technical Considerations,* multimedia content is tied to a number of issues that limit its usefulness on educational sites. When dealing with multimedia forms, copyright is a concern. Many of the multimedia items found on the Web are not used with the permission of the owners and are in violation of copyright. If streaming audio and video are captioned for accessibility, obtain written permission before the captions are created. Captioning is a form of adaptation, and the right to make or authorize adaptations is reserved to the copyright holder. Accessibility can also be an issue due to the need for plug-ins and long download times. Some districts may restrict the use of multimedia content for these reasons and because of the tremendous amount of server space they require. Multimedia formats include streaming audio, downloadable audio, streaming video, downloadable video, video conferencing, chat, and PowerPoint or HyperStudio presentations.

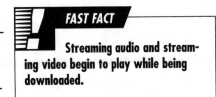

FAST FACT

Streaming audio and streaming video begin to play while being downloaded.

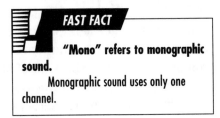

FAST FACT

"Mono" refers to monographic sound.
Monographic sound uses only one channel.

As when using images, try to minimize download times. Record in mono instead of stereo to cut the sizes of audio files. Sampling rates can be set lower, as can sound resolution (use eight bits instead of sixteen). Begin to minimize video download times by reducing screen sizes to a fraction (1/4 or 1/2) of the full screen size. Cut the number of frames per second and limit colors. Downloading these kinds of files should always be optional, never automatic. Help users make informed choices by indicating the length of the piece to be downloaded.

▶ WHEN TO BREAK THE RULES

Local Web planners know best the audience that their Web pages are intended to serve. Maybe the page is being written for primary students. In that case, using a larger font than the recommended size would be a necessity. To make the site appeal to middle school students, include some animated .gifs and other funky and tacky "stuff." If the page is being used to showcase student work, consider pages with backgrounds, layouts, and colors that are inconsistent with the rest of the Web site. Perhaps the Web site is a teaching tool. For example, if students need to learn how to scroll, make pages longer than the suggested three to five screens.

➤ BREAKING THE RULES!

It is important to remember that many Web sites have a global audience. Following a few rules can ensure that an educational Web site shows an educational institution in the best possible light. It is possible to find list after list of design tips, design "do's," and design "don'ts" on the Internet and in books. But keep in mind that top designers do not always agree on what those "rules" are. In other words, the rules are not universal. One notable designer may blast the idea of including text labels with image maps, while 20 others (and accessibility experts) may list those labels as design musts.

While being aware of the global nature of the Web, local Web planners also need to think of their targeted audiences when making design decisions. That can mean breaking or at least bending a few rules. Some rules, such as copyright and district Web publishing rules, are not negotiable—breaking or even bending them is not acceptable. At times, other types of rules need to and should be broken to meet the needs of the users. Just make certain you know the basic rules and have a defensible reason for breaking them. Design impacts a great deal more than the look of a Web site. Good design decisions result in Web sites that are accessible, easy to use, readable, and pleasing to the eye.

➤ IS IT DONE YET?

Will the planned design work? Use the *Design Check Sheet* and the *Web Site Evaluation Form* in **Appendix 1** to evaluate sample Web page templates. Also, test templates on a variety of computers and an assortment of browsers before spending large amounts of time entering information. If possible, involve stakeholders in selecting details for the final look. This can be as informal as showing groups of students or teachers two different backgrounds and asking their opinion on which looks best. While checking your design against the design guidelines, remember that sometimes a little judicious bending of the design guidelines is necessary to meet the needs of the targeted users.

When a site seems to be ready to be placed on the Internet, take time to thoroughly check it before loading it to the Web. Use the *Prepublication Check Sheet* in **Appendix 1** to check the site. Take the site to a variety of browsers and computers. When doing final evaluations, look for design and content errors. Print pages and ask several proofreaders to find spelling and grammar errors. Copy Web site text, paste into a word processing program, and run grammar and spell checks. Or use Web tools designed for this purpose. Invite "new eyes," people who have not seen the site, to proofread and look for mistakes. Challenge students to find mistakes or offer rewards to students who find mistakes. Ask members of the targeted audience to test the site on their computers. Ask design-related questions such as "Did you have any problems with finding the pages on the site?" or "Was it readable?" Find out if colors or graphics are causing any problems.

Revisit the *Design Check Sheet* in **Appendix 1** to evaluate the results. Test the Web site every possible way before loading it on the server and announcing it to the world. When the Web site has been checked and rechecked and is something to be proud of, publish it on the Web.

Chapter 10

The Never-ending Journey

Never ending, still beginning...

—*John Dryden*

Okay, the site is now on the Web. Is it done yet? No . . .it is just beginning. Now it is time to let the world, or at least the intended audience(s), know where the site is and how to use it. The work does not stop with promotion and education; maintenance, evaluation, and revision are also ongoing aspects of Web work.

▶ PROMOTION

Once a Web site has been built and is on the Web, the next step is to make certain that targeted groups utilize the site. The Internet has literally billions of pages. The intended primary and secondary audiences need to be made aware of what the site has to offer so that they want to find and use the Web site. The targeted groups also need to be shown where and how to locate the site. It is time to promote the Web site. Because target audiences and their needs have already been identified and studied, the resulting information can be utilized to create a carefully tailored promotion plan. **See** *Promotion Check Sheet* in **Appendix 1**.

Will publicity need to be aimed toward audiences within the school system or to groups outside the school system? Share information about the site in the school or district using promotions such as newsletters, letters,

> **QUICK TIP**
>
> Have the Web address printed on bookmarks, fliers, brochures, newsletters, business cards, and other forms of printed materials. Send bookmarks home with students. Offer the business cards to administrators, community members, parents, and other educators. Staff members may want copies of business cards to hand out.

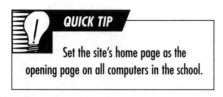

QUICK TIP

Set the site's home page as the opening page on all computers in the school.

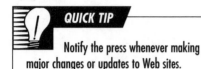

QUICK TIP

Notify the press whenever making major changes or updates to Web sites.

announcements, inservice sessions, bulletin boards, bookmarks, business cards, and "grand opening" events. If parents or other community members are among the targeted group, promote the Web site through newsletters, letters, announcements at events, bookmarks, business cards, radio stories, newspaper articles, television reports, and other publicity devices. **See** *Promotion Check Sheet* in **Appendix 1**. Instruction on how to use the Web site is an effective promotional tool for all types of audience. Educational sessions or how-to handouts can raise awareness while providing instruction.

Working with the Press

If working with the media, one of the most effective ways to get their attention is to invite them to the school to see the Web site being used. Time the invitation to coincide with the presence of

---

WRITING A PRESS RELEASE

INCLUDE THE FOLLOWING IN THE PRESS RELEASE:

- The school's/district's name and logo
- Contact person's name and phone number (upper right hand corner of page)
- A release date
- A catchy "headline"/title, which the news organization may or may not use

USE THESE TIPS WHEN WRITING THE PRESS RELEASE:

- Begin with a strong opening sentence that will draw in the reader and embody the message.
- Start with the most important information, using the inverted-pyramid style of writing.
- Include a brief (three-or-four sentence) explanation of the story that answers the traditional journalistic questions: who, what, where, when, why, and how.
- Use the active voice.
- Use the third person.
- Avoid educational and technical jargon.
- Include quotes.
- Use concise, simple sentences.
- Make it accurate, exciting, and interesting.
- Include information about your organization at the end.
- End with one of the following in parentheses:
    three pound signs (###)
    the word "end" in capital letters (END)
    the number thirty (30).

ACCOMPANYING PHOTOS SHOULD DO THE FOLLOWING:

- Show action
- Include names (check school policy regarding the release of student photos to the press)
- Be labeled with identifying information, including names

Note: *Send to a specific reporter, managing editor, or news director.*

students, teachers, or invited guests who are using the Web site at the time of the visit. Members of the media like having opportunities to take action pictures or video. Present press representative(s) with a prepared information sheet. On the sheet include the reasons for the Web site. Indicate how the Web site will help meet the needs of targeted users. Identify the individuals involved in the creation of the Web site. When the story is reported, bear in mind that press coverage is good even if a story is not entirely accurate. Write thank-you notes when a reporter makes a special effort to cover a story, even if the story does not exactly reflect what has happened. Parents, administrators, other educators, and the public will have a better idea of possible roles of educational Web sites.

Making Search Engine Hit Lists

Listing Web sites on Internet search engines and tools is a form of promotion that is unique to the Internet. Having a Web site listed by search engines/tools is one of the first steps to help connect targeted users to a Web site. Submission information can be found on search engine Web sites. Each tool has specific procedures for indexing submitted Web sites. Follow any directions provided when submitting sites. Some types of information that are commonly requested include the site's name, a Web address, an author's name, a brief description (might specify number of words permitted), keywords, and the most appropriate topic. In addition to notifying search tools about the site, contact educational directories. Many have submission

QUICK TIP

Make a checklist of all of the major search engines (e.g., Google, Yahoo, AltaVista) to use as a guide for submissions.

QUICK TIP

Be sure to place the title of a Web page at the top of the page. Placing the title at the top of a page will improve how some search tools list a web page.

FAST FACT

META tags are used to record Web site keywords, the title, a description, and the author.

This information can be found in the code portion of a Web site. Some search engines search for META tags, while others do not. Careful wording of META tags can help some search engines to better categorize and identify a Web site.

When writing META tag keywords, choose words that reflect each page's content. Including a few more general words is also helpful. Specific phrases that match a page's content can be effective. If one of the keywords is commonly misspelled, include the misspelled version. The number of characters that can be put into META tags is limited, so pick the best words and phrases. Check search engine help pages for suggestions on how to optimize the use of META tags.

RESOURCE BOX

META TAGS

About.com: Meta Tags
<http://html.miningco.com/compute/html/cs/metatags/index.htm>
This site provides Meta tag guides and links to other recommended Meta tag sites.

A Dictionary of HTML Meta Data Tags
<http://vancouver-webpages.com/META/metatags.detail.html>
This dictionary gives detailed and sophisticated information about the various Meta tags.

Search Engine Watch: How to Use HTML Meta Tags
<http://www.SearchEngineWatch.com/webmasters/meta.html>
In addition to giving an easy-to-understand explanation of Meta tags, this site includes links to other Web pages that explain Meta tags.

10 Questions About Meta Data
<http://www.builder.com/Authoring/Metadata/?dd.bu.bb.0909.02>
This site presents information on subjects related to Meta tags and the indexing of Web pages.

processes similar to those of traditional search engines. Tools and sites are available that simultaneously submit Web sites to multiple search tools. However, these tools are often not as effective as directly submitting pages to specific tools.

▶ EDUCATION

Awareness of a Web site is not meaningful if targeted audiences are unable to utilize it. Some intended audiences may need assistance and education before they can use the Web site. During the Web planning team's research process, the team gathered information about intended audiences. Use this information to plan and possibly budget for training. The amount and nature of training required depend on factors such as the intended users, their sophistication, and the type of Web site and pages. Education may range from short and informal to extended and structured. Users may need no instruction, a simple instructional sheet, or face-to-face, direct instruction. The Web site itself can be designed to be a kind of teaching tool. It might include a tutorial or links to tutorials. Trainers can be staff members, outside consultants, or even students. As trainers provide instruction, they can start the evaluation process by noting which aspects of the site are confusing, helpful, difficult, easy, and so forth. Once a Web site is available and being used, take the evaluation process to the next level.

▶ EVALUATION

Evaluation is not limited to checking a site before publishing it on a Web—it is an ongoing process. How a Web site is evaluated is determined by what information is needed about the Web site. **See** *Evaluation Planning Sheet* in **Appendix 1**. Evaluation tools can include traditional Web site evaluation forms, surveys, and interviews. Observations of use patterns are also meaningful. Tracking software can indicate when, how, and to a certain extent, who is using a Web site.

When creating or selecting effective evaluation tools, think about what information is needed and how it will be used. **See** *Web Site Evaluation Form* in **Appendix 1**. Consider the types of information that could impact funding, support, updates, and revisions. Are statistics needed? Is feedback about usability important? Are some sections of the Web site being used heavily or not being used at all? Is content effective? Once information is gathered, use it. Make sure that Web teams, administrators, and the public are aware of successes. Look at negative comments as learning tools. Use them to plan improvements and revisions.

▶ MAINTENANCE

Web site evaluation and maintenance go hand in hand. Deliberate and systematic Web site maintenance is crucial to having a high-quality Web site. Web sites never achieve a "done" status. Having a Web site is like having a baby. A Web site never grows out of needing care and attention. Web sites appear, disappear, and change drastically at an incredible rate. Links that were created yesterday may not work today. Have a schedule for keeping links updated. A link-checking tool can be an excellent resource. Even if a link-checking tool is being used, occasionally check links manually. URLs can be sold, and the nature of pages new to URLs may not be appropriate for educational Web sites. Check that the link name matches the name of the page found at the URL.

An "Adopt-A-Page" program, in which students adopt pages, is a good way to maintain a large Web site. Students and volunteers who adopt pages agree to check pages regularly and to report any broken links. Maintenance also includes making other minor corrections, additions, and updates as needed. For example, game scores can be added moments after sporting events. While maintaining the site, constantly evaluate the effectiveness of the Web site as a resource. **See** *Maintenance Check Sheet* in **Appendix 1**.

▷ REVISION

The web is fluid. Like an ocean, its shape and look is constantly changing. Appearances and practices that are "cutting edge" today probably will be dated in a matter of months. A Web site is never done. Informed and meaningful changes should be constant. Use evaluation information as one indicator for making revision decisions. At least one Web team member needs to actively monitor information on the changes in Web publishing and technologies.

Appendix 1:
Web Planning and Check Sheets

District Web Planning Team Information Sheet

School Web Planning Team Information Sheet

Web Site Vision Statement Worksheet

Technical Support Resource List

Publishing Guidelines and Policies Check Sheet

Web Team Decision-Planning Sheet: Questions to
Consider When Making Recommendations and Setting Goals

Web Site Goals Worksheet

Web Site Objectives Worksheet

Informative Educational Web Pages Planning Sheet

Curricular Pages Planning Sheet

Showcase Pages Planning Sheet

Revenue Generation Pages Planning Sheet

Evaluating Web Sites for Linking

Copyright Check Sheet

Technical Considerations & Constraints Check Sheet

Design Check Sheet

File Name Worksheet

Image Source Note Sheet

Prepublication Check Sheet

Promotion Check Sheet

Evaluation Planning Sheet

Web Site Evaluation Form

Maintenance Check Sheet

DISTRICT WEB PLANNING TEAM INFORMATION SHEET

Team Coordinator _____

District Administrator _____

Board Member/Trustee _____

Principal _____

Librarian/Media Specialist _____

Teacher _____

Computer Technician/Technology Coordinator _____

District Computer/Server Technician _____

School Computer/Server Technician _____

Security/Legal Advisor _____

Public or Media Relations Department Representative _____

Parent _____

Community Member _____

Alumni _____

SCHOOL WEB PLANNING TEAM INFORMATION SHEET

Team Coordinator _____

Principal _____

Librarian/Media Specialist _____

Computer Technician/Technology Coordinator _____

Teachers/Staff:

Student(s):

Parent(s):

Community Member(s):

Alumni:

Reproducible from *K–12 Web Pages: Planning & Publishing Excellent School Web Sites* by Debra Kay Logan and Cynthia Beuselinck (Linworth Publishing, Inc., 2002)

WEB SITE VISION STATEMENT WORKSHEET

Project name: _____   Date: ____/____/____

1 What are the underlying reasons for the Web site? What is/are the purpose(s) of a Web site? Why should a Web site be created?

_____

_____

_____

_____

_____

_____

2 What is the primary audience that the Web site is intended to reach?

_____

3 List the targeted secondary or additional audiences for the Web site in order of priority.

1. _____   2. _____

3. _____   4. _____

5. _____   6. _____

7. _____   8. _____

4 Identify any special needs (ability levels, learning needs, accessibility requirements, cultural sensitivities, or community issues) of the Web site's targeted audiences.

_____

_____

_____

_____

_____

_____

Reproducible from *K–12 Web Pages: Planning & Publishing Excellent School Web Sites* by Debra Kay Logan and Cynthia Beuselinck (Linworth Publishing, Inc., 2002)

WEB SITE VISION STATEMENT WORKSHEET continued

Project name: _____

Date:

_____/_____/_____

5 Identify priorities and special interests of the targeted groups.

_____

_____

_____

_____

_____

6 Identify types of Web pages and Web resources that might best serve the needs of the intended audiences.

_____

_____

_____

_____

_____

_____

_____

_____

7 Write a **Vision Statement** that in three or fewer sentences tells the purpose of the Web site, its primary audience, and how the Web site will function and accomplish its purpose. The statement should be clear, yet broad enough to allow for creativity.

_____

_____

_____

TECHNICAL SUPPORT RESOURCE LIST

Project name: _____   Date: ____/____/____

WEB SERVER

- ☐ Located at district offices
  Technical support contact: _____
- ☐ Located within school
  Technical support contact: _____
- ☐ Located with external provider
  Technical support contact: _____

TRAINING RESOURCES

- ☐ District-supplied   ☐ School-supplied   ☐ Combination
- ☐ Instructor-led   ☐ Online

District-level contact: _____

Local school contact: _____
Details:

SECURITY

- ☐ Security Advisor   ☐ Security Team

District level contact: _____

Local school contact: _____

LOADING RESPONSIBILITIES

- ☐ District loading all pages

  Contact: _____

- ☐ School loading own pages

  Contact: _____

  School password holders: _____

  _____

Reproducible from *K–12 Web Pages: Planning & Publishing Excellent School Web Sites* by Debra Kay Logan and Cynthia Beuselinck (Linworth Publishing, Inc., 2002)

TECHNICAL SUPPORT RESOURCE LIST continued

CHANGE CONTROLS

Team member status checked: ☐ monthly   ☐ annually   ☐ other

District contact for changes: _____

Local contact for changes: _____

PRIMARY CONTACTS FOR EXPERTISE

Team training: _____

Policy & procedural updates: _____

Graphics & layout: _____

Scripting/coding: _____

Storyboarding: _____

Classroom projects: _____

Cool/new tools: _____

Other: _____

POLICY & GUIDELINES TEAM/COMMITTEE

District team members:

Local team members:

CONTENT TEAM/COMMITTEE

District team members:

Local team members:

CHALLENGES CONTACT: _____

Reproducible from *K–12 Web Pages: Planning & Publishing Excellent School Web Sites* by Debra Kay Logan and Cynthia Beuselinck (Linworth Publishing, Inc., 2002)

PUBLISHING GUIDELINES AND POLICIES CHECK SHEET

Project name: _____   Date: _____/_____/_____

DESIGN FEATURES

1 Required header

2 Required footer

3 Pages that must be linked

4 Copyright format

5 Author and contact formats

6 Date formats

7 Logo usage information

8 Limitations on graphics/multimedia

Reproducible from *K–12 Web Pages: Planning & Publishing Excellent School Web Sites* by Debra Kay Logan and Cynthia Beuselinck (Linworth Publishing, Inc., 2002)

PUBLISHING GUIDELINES AND POLICIES CHECK SHEET continued

9 Restricted file types

10 Requirements for accessibility

CONTENT REQUIREMENTS

1 Public content that must be available

2 Content that will be available only on the Intranet

3 Content that will not be posted on the site

4 Extracurricular groups permitted   ☐ Yes   ☐ No

5 Criteria for inclusion as external group

6 Restrictions on content by external groups

7 Restrictions on content produced by students

PUBLISHING GUIDELINES AND POLICIES CHECK SHEET continued

8 Restrictions on content produced by staff

9 Restrictions on commercial links and content

10 Maintenance requirements for pages

11 Retention periods for pages (varies depending on content)

12 Archiving policy and required formats

SAFETY AND LIABILITY POLICIES

1 Personal information permitted

☐ Staff full names   Format: _____

☐ Staff e-mail addresses

☐ Staff photographs

☐ Student names   Format: _____

☐ Student photographs

☐ Other (describe)

2 Personal information not permitted

PUBLISHING GUIDELINES AND POLICIES CHECK SHEET continued

3 Location of permission forms for personal information

4 Publishing student work

☐ As selected by teachers   ☐ Only best student work

5 Location of permission forms for student work

6 Location of forms or form letters for copyright release of external works

RESPONSIBILITY ASSIGNMENTS TO BE INCLUDED IN GUIDELINES AND POLICIES

Uploading done by: _____

Proofreading done by: _____

Content challenges handled by: _____

Web files maintained by: _____

Technical structure defined by: _____

WEB PUBLISHING GUIDELINE AND POLICY REVIEWS

Review done by: _____

Review schedule: _____

Date: _____/_____/_____

1 Who will work on the site and what compensation will they receive?

Team leader _____

Web designer(s) _____

Graphics creator _____

Content author _____

Web page builder _____

2 What types of software and other tools will Web authors need?

Web authoring/HTML tools _____

Graphics tools _____

Compression tools _____

Site maintenance tools _____

Digital cameras _____

Scanners _____

Other _____

3 What types of team training will be needed?

Use of authoring and image tools_____

Policies and safe practices_____

Copyright_____

Web design_____

4 What provisions will be necessary for training?

Who will provide training? _____

Where will training be provided? _____

How will the cost of training be addressed? _____

WEB TEAM DECISION-PLANNING SHEET: QUESTIONS TO CONSIDER WHEN MAKING RECOMMENDATIONS AND SETTING GOALS continued

5 What types of pages will be included on the site?

Use *Page Planning Sheets* in **Appendix 1.**

How will information be organized? _____

How will information be grouped? _____

6 What kinds of content will be found on the pages?

Use *Page Planning Sheets* in **Appendix 1.**

7 What types of signed permissions will be required? _____

_____

8 Who will be responsible for approving content before a Web page is loaded to the server? _____

9 By what date will the initial Web site be on the Web? _____

10 How will the site be publicized:

A. in the building and district?
- ☐ newsletters
- ☐ letters
- ☐ public announcements
- ☐ inservice training
- ☐ bulletin boards
- ☐ bookmarks
- ☐ other _____

B. in the community?
- ☐ newsletters
- ☐ newspapers
- ☐ radio
- ☐ television
- ☐ links from other community sites
- ☐ workshops
- ☐ other _____

C. on the Web?

☐ submission to search engines

☐ notify online educational resource sites

☐ other _____

11 Will instruction on how to use the site be needed? If so:

Who will need to be trained? _____

How will they be notified? _____

Who will do the training? _____

When will the training be? _____

Where will the training be? _____

12 How and when will the Web site be maintained and updated? _____

_____

13 How often will links be tested? _____

14 How will the site be evaluated? _____

WEB SITE GOALS WORKSHEET

Date: _____/_____/_____

	_____TERM/RANGE GOALS	RESPONSIBLE PERSON(S)	DATE DUE/ COMPLETED
1.			
2.			
3.			
4.			
5.			
6.			
7.			
8.			
9.			
10.			
11.			
12.			

REVIEW SCHEDULE: MONTHLY–REVIEW DATE:_____

ANNUALLY–REVIEW DATE:_____

Reproducible from *K–12 Web Pages: Planning & Publishing Excellent School Web Sites* by Debra Kay Logan and Cynthia Beuselinck (Linworth Publishing, Inc., 2002)

WEB SITE OBJECTIVES WORKSHEET

Date: _____ / _____ / _____

CORRES-PONDING GOAL	OBJECTIVE NUMBER	OBJECTIVES	PERSON RESPONSIBLE	EVIDENCE THAT OBJECTIVE IS BEING MET	DATE DUE/ COMPLETED

REVIEW SCHEDULE: MONTHLY–REVIEW DATE:_____

ANNUALLY–REVIEW DATE:_____

Reproducible from *K–12 Web Pages: Planning & Publishing Excellent School Web Sites* by Debra Kay Logan and Cynthia Beuselinck (Linworth Publishing, Inc., 2002)

INFORMATIVE EDUCATIONAL WEB PAGES PLANNING SHEET

Date: _____ / _____ / _____

PRIORITY		NOTES
	Contact information*	
	■ directory	
	■ individual's school phone numbers	
	■ staff e-mail addresses	
	■ fax numbers	
	■ who to call for help	
	Mission statement	
	Letter/greeting from the superintendent, principal, teacher, other	
	Goals & objectives	
	Strategic or other long-term plans	
	Locations (maps)*	
	Hours	
	Pictures of building(s)	
	Information about mandated testing	
	Accreditation	
	District/school history	
	Symbols (motto, logo, mascot, other)	
	Demographics	
	Staff statistics/professional biographies*	
	Registration procedures and materials	
	Fees	
	Supply lists	
	Menus	
	Weather and other emergency procedure information	
	Board meeting agendas and open session minutes	

Reproducible from *K–12 Web Pages: Planning & Publishing Excellent School Web Sites* by Debra Kay Logan and Cynthia Beuselinck (Linworth Publishing, Inc., 2002)

INFORMATIVE EDUCATIONAL WEB PAGES PLANNING SHEET continued

	Committee information and possibly minutes	
	Budget information	
	Vendor information	
	Job postings	
	Alumni information	
	reunion information	
	famous alumni	
	contact forms	
	Newsletters- stories and information about what is happening in the district, school, department, classroom	
	Awards & honors*	
	Bus route/transportation information*	
	Calendar/Time line*	
	■ school year with holidays & breaks	
	■ sports with scores	
	■ special events	
	■ field trips	
	■ units of study	
	■ assignment due dates	
	■ testing	
	Curriculum overview	
	Student handbook	
	Policies and procedures	
	■ dress code	
	■ homework	
	■ discipline	
	■ attendance	
	■ expectations/rules	
	■ drug policy	
	Online grade book and final grades	

Reproducible from *K–12 Web Pages: Planning & Publishing Excellent School Web Sites* by Debra Kay Logan and Cynthia Beuselinck (Linworth Publishing, Inc., 2002)

INFORMATIVE EDUCATIONAL WEB PAGES PLANNING SHEET continued

	Attendance records	
	Information sheets and permission forms for parents	
	Special services	
	Special programs	
	Graduation requirements	
	College credit opportunities	
	Scholarship information and resources	
	Extracurricular activities/school-sponsored clubs	
	Volunteer requests	
	PTA/PTO information	
	Wish lists	
	Volunteer information	
	Links to local/community resources and services	
	Links to parenting resources	
	Helpful tips and other original information	
	Educational research findings	
	Feedback resources for comments, suggestions, other	
	e-mail	
	forms	
	surveys	
	guest book	
	listserv	
	bulletin board	
	discussion groups	
	Resource lists/databases	
	Other	
	Other	
	Other	

* Look at safety considerations/district Web publishing policy before posting this kind of information.

Reproducible from *K–12 Web Pages: Planning & Publishing Excellent School Web Sites* by Debra Kay Logan and Cynthia Beuselinck (Linworth Publishing, Inc., 2002)

CURRICULAR PAGES PLANNING SHEET

Date: _____/_____/_____

PRIORITY		NOTES
	Standards, objectives, and outcomes	
	Assignments, handouts, rubrics, check sheets, test, and due dates	
	Vocabulary and/or spelling lists*	
	Reading lists	
	Project page	
	Pathfinders	
	Scavenger hunts	
	Fact page or article	
	Tutorial simulation	
	Virtual tour or museum	
	Practice test	
	Puzzles	
	Gateway/e-library/hot links	
	Webquests/research investigation	
	Collaborative projects	
	Educational lesson archive	
	Educational tips	
	Educational articles	

* Look at safety considerations/district Web publishing policy before posting this kind of information.

Reproducible from *K–12 Web Pages: Planning & Publishing Excellent School Web Sites* by Debra Kay Logan and Cynthia Beuselinck (Linworth Publishing, Inc., 2002)

SHOWCASE PAGES PLANNING SHEET*

Date: _____ / _____ / _____

REMINDER: When posting student works, check and follow policy before using student names. Have and use copyright release form.

PRIORITY	WORK TO SHOWCASE:	NOTES
	■ Artwork	
	■ Poetry	
	■ Composition/prose	
	■ Articles	
	■ Newsletters	
	■ Newspapers	
	■ Reports	
	■ Multimedia presentations	
	■ Web sites	
	■ Collaborative projects	
	■ Student portfolio	
	■ Class portfolio	

* Look at safety considerations/district Web publishing policy before posting this kind of information.

Reproducible from *K–12 Web Pages: Planning & Publishing Excellent School Web Sites* by Debra Kay Logan and Cynthia Beuselinck (Linworth Publishing, Inc., 2002)

REVENUE GENERATION PAGES PLANNING SHEET

Date: _____ / _____ / _____

PRIORITY		NOTES
	Online auctions	
	Affiliate programs	
	Shop-to-give programs	
	Online charity programs	
	Other	

* Look at safety considerations/district Web Publishing policy before posting this kind of information.

Reproducible from *K–12 Web Pages: Planning & Publishing Excellent School Web Sites* by Debra Kay Logan and Cynthia Beuselinck (Linworth Publishing, Inc., 2002)

EVALUATING WEB SITES FOR LINKING

Date: _____ / _____ / _____

Site name:	URL: http://			
CRITERIA:	**UNACCEPTABLE**	**POOR**	**GOOD**	**EXCELLENT**
IS THE SITE RELEVANT?				
IS THE SITE AGE-APPROPRIATE FOR INTENDED USE? CHECK THE:				
Readability				
Concept load				
Appeal				
IS THE CONTENT:				
Original?				
Accurate?				
Complete?				
Unbiased/objective?				
Clear?				
Current?				
Unique?				
Appealing?				
Are the links appropriate?				
Do the links work?				
Are graphics meaningful?				
Commercial content does not interfere with information.				
IS THE AUTHOR AN AUTHORITY?				
Is the site signed?				
Are the author's credentials provided?				
Can information and credentials be verified?				
Are sources credited?				
Is the sponsoring organization identified (if appropriate)?				
Is contact information given?				

Reproducible from *K–12 Web Pages: Planning & Publishing Excellent School Web Sites* by Debra Kay Logan and Cynthia Beuselinck (Linworth Publishing, Inc., 2002)

EVALUATING WEB SITES FOR LINKING continued

Identify the **type of site**: .com, .net, .ac, .edu, .k12, .org, .gov, .mil				
EXAMINE THE FORMAT FOR:				
Accessibility				
Download speed				
Ease of navigation				
Searchability				
Functionality/usability				
Aesthetic appeal				
Instructions or help provided?				
TOTALS:				

SELECTED: ☐ YES ☐ NO

COPYRIGHT CHECK SHEET

Date: _____/_____/_____

MATERIALS USED ON THE WEB SITE:

1 Original

- ☐ District/school has written permission.
- ☐ Permissions are filed in a permission folder.
- ☐ Use restrictions (if any) are identified and followed.
- ☐ Credit is given on the Web site.

2 Commercial or from online sources

- ☐ District/school has written permission.
- ☐ Permissions are filed in a permission folder.
- ☐ Use restrictions (if any) are identified and followed.
- ☐ Credit is given on the Web site.
- ☐ Fees (if any) are paid.

3 Student-created

- ☐ Used within the framework of the district's Web publishing policies/guidelines.
- ☐ Used only with written permission of the student and guardian.

LINKS & HTML

1 ☐ Not copied from a compiled list

2 If using frames:

- ☐ The user is given the option of turning off frames or opening links in a new window.
- ☐ It is made clear to the user that the linked-to site is not part of the site's content.

3 ☐ Deep links are avoided if the webmaster requests no deep linking.

4 ☐ Permission is obtained and saved in a permission folder before logos are used as links.

5 ☐ Links are not made to sites that violate copyright.

- ☐ Optional: ☐ Webmasters are sent e-mails indicating intent to link.
  - ☐ Responses to link e-mails are filed.

Reproducible from *K–12 Web Pages: Planning & Publishing Excellent School Web Sites* by Debra Kay Logan and Cynthia Beuselinck (Linworth Publishing, Inc., 2002)

COPYRIGHT CHECK SHEET continued

6 Only short passages of HTML or other code are copied.

ONLINE SERVICE PROVIDERS' LIABILITY

1 ☐ Legal assistance and advice is sought to meet and follow requirements.

2 ☐ A copyright agent is registered with the copyright office.

3 ☐ The copyright agent's name is posted along with the district's copyright policy on the OSP's (district's or school's) Web site.

PROTECTING WEB SITES

1 Every page displays copyright information:

☐ Copyright, Copr., or ©

☐ Year first published/current year

☐ Name of the copyright holder

2 ☐ Optional: Web site is registered with the copyright office.

3 Possible ways to bury clues for locating plagiarized sites:

☐ Unique text is deliberately included.

☐ Unusual links are buried in the site.

☐ META tags are included in the page coding.

☐ Intentional misspellings are hidden in the site (not recommended for educational Web sites).

☐ Images are given unique name(s).

☐ Images are watermarked.

Reproducible from *K–12 Web Pages: Planning & Publishing Excellent School Web Sites* by Debra Kay Logan and Cynthia Beuselinck (Linworth Publishing, Inc., 2002)

TECHNICAL CONSIDERATIONS & CONSTRAINTS CHECK SHEET

Date: ____/____/____

WEB SERVER

☐ Macintosh ☐ WebStar ☐ Microsoft IIS ☐ Apache

☐ Netscape ☐ IBM WebSphere ☐ Other

HOSTING LOCATION

☐ District server(s) ☐ Local server(s) ☐ ISP ☐ Other

SPACE ALLOCATIONS

Amount of space available for use on the server

_____

Methods to be employed to use server space effectively:

SERVER & BANDWIDTH RESTRICTIONS

Default home page file name required on the server _____

Bandwidth limitations _____

LOADING RESTRICTIONS

☐ Size of graphics details: _____

☐ Multimedia files details: _____

☐ Programs details: _____

Other:

SPECIAL FEATURES AVAILABLE

☐ Forms handler

☐ Hit counter

☐ Database connectivity

☐ Specialized software support (e.g., FrontPage extensions, Cold Fusion, UltraDev)

☐ Other

To use special scripts, contact: _____

DESIGN CHECK SHEET

Date: _____/_____/_____

BASICS . . . GET READY TO DESIGN

A Look at targeted end users and intended use. Identify any special needs:

B Explore Web evaluation forms.

C Shop for ideas by looking at other Web sites. Create a file or notebook of design ideas.

ACCESS

A **Accessibility**

1. Who will be using the site? _____
_____

2. What kind(s) of equipment are involved? _____
_____

3. Which browsers are being used? _____

4. Graphics are made more accessible by:
   - ☐ using as few graphics as possible
   - ☐ using ALT attributes with periods at the end for graphics
   - ☐ using thumbnails in place of larger images on main pages
   - ☐ using text links as alternatives to image maps
   - ☐ avoiding plug-ins if possible
   - ☐ captioning streaming video and audio files if permission is given by the copyright holder
   - ☐ avoiding extensive use of JavaScript if users utilize older equipment and browsers

5. Tables are made more accessible by:
   - a. ☐ using Cascading Style Sheets instead of tables for design
   - b. labeling the table by:
     - ☐ giving it a title
     - ☐ using descriptive notes to use in caption elements
     - ☐ explaining its structure and purpose in summaries attributes

6. The accessibility of forms is increased by:
   - ☐ writing descriptive text for input areas
   - ☐ labeling buttons and other controls
   - ☐ grouping form options

Reproducible from *K–12 Web Pages: Planning & Publishing Excellent School Web Sites* by Debra Kay Logan and Cynthia Beuselinck (Linworth Publishing, Inc., 2002)

DESIGN CHECK SHEET continued

B **Site Structure**

1. Storyboard, chart, or list various possible arrangements of planned pages.

   _____

   _____

2. Experiment with arrangements of pages:
   - ☐ Hierarchical
   - ☐ Web or Interconnected
   - ☐ Tutorial
   - ☐ Combination

C **Navigation**

1. Every page is linked to home page.
2. Navigation menus all have:
   - ☐ consistent look
   - ☐ consistent location
   - ☐ clear link titles
   - ☐ location on opening screen of the home page
3. Pages are no longer than three to five screens.
4. Long pages have menus:
   - ☐ at the top of the page with descriptive links to portions of the page
   - ☐ that include "back to the top" links

D **Layout**

Page layout is achieved through the use of tools and techniques such as:

1. ☐ page planning map
2. ☐ template
3. ☐ tables (check accessibility issues)
4. ☐ Cascading Style Sheets
5. ☐ horizontal design of home page
6. ☐ consistent:
   - a. ☐ backgrounds
   - b. ☐ colors
   - c. ☐ images
   - d. ☐ arrangement/placement of:
     - ☐ logos
     - ☐ headings

DESIGN CHECK SHEET continued

- ☐ navigation
- ☐ tools/menu
- ☐ background images (if any)
- ☐ content
- ☐ contact/responsibility information
- ☐ copyright notice
- ☐ update information

FORMATS

Ⓐ Images

1. Image download time is minimized by:
   - ☐ keeping total file sizes under 30 to 35 KB
   - ☐ limiting numbers of images
   - ☐ using thumbnails
   - ☐ reusing the same images
   - ☐ designating image size with Web editor or HTML
   - ☐ keeping banners small

2. Image "Do's and Don'ts":

   a. Avoid or judiciously use:
   - ☐ animated gifs
   - ☐ image bars
   - ☐ scrolling text
   - ☐ flashing or blinking text
   - ☐ counter

   b. Do:
   - ☐ coordinate image colors to total page
   - ☐ credit sources
   - ☐ use ALT attributes
   - ☐ check use guidelines

Ⓑ Colors

1. Use colors that are:
   - ☐ Web-safe
   - ☐ readable
   - ☐ attractive
   - ☐ consistent

Reproducible from *K–12 Web Pages: Planning & Publishing Excellent School Web Sites* by Debra Kay Logan and Cynthia Beuselinck (Linworth Publishing, Inc., 2002)

DESIGN CHECK SHEET continued

2. Make certain that:
- [ ] gray is used judiciously
- [ ] there is a high contrast between text and background (preferably dark on light)
- [ ] colors are not sending inappropriate cultural messages
- [ ] colors send appropriate emotional messages

C **Text**

1. [ ] Type is limited to 25% to 30% of the Web page.
2. [ ] Lines of type on a page are no wider than width of a book.
3. [ ] Lines are 40 to 60 characters per line of text or 30 to 40 characters per line of text in columns.
4. [ ] Font size is between 10 and 14 points.
5. [ ] All fonts are the same or are from the same font family.
6. [ ] Text is aligned to the left and not centered or justified.
7. [ ] Text is upper and lower case letters.
8. [ ] Paragraphs are short.
9. [ ] Bulleted and numbered lists are used to highlight information.
10. [ ] Blank lines are used between paragraphs.
11. Information is highlighted by:
- [ ] putting borders around it
- [ ] placing it the upper left corner of the page
- [ ] locating it one-third of the way down the page on the right
- [ ] using, but not overusing, bold and italics
- [ ] utilizing headings, subheadings, lines, and color

CONTENT

A **Quality**
- [ ] relevant
- [ ] reliable
- [ ] accurate
- [ ] complete
- [ ] objective
- [ ] clear
- [ ] current
- [ ] unique
- [ ] appealing

Reproducible from *K–12 Web Pages: Planning & Publishing Excellent School Web Sites* by Debra Kay Logan and Cynthia Beuselinck (Linworth Publishing, Inc., 2002)

DESIGN CHECK SHEET continued

B **Links**
- [ ] selected with the vision in mind
- [ ] evaluated for inclusion
- [ ] organized
- [ ] annotated (including page title and URL)

C **Writing**
- [ ] easy to scan
- [ ] in the inverted pyramid style
- [ ] simple and brief
- [ ] in an active or imperative voice
- [ ] shows awareness of the global audience
- [ ] spelled correctly
- [ ] grammatically correct

A **Multimedia**
- [ ] formats are selected for accessibility
- [ ] file size is minimized
- [ ] plug-ins are available and compatible with users' resources

ESSENTIAL PAGE ELEMENTS

A Every educational Web **site** should include **authority** information such as:
- [ ] links to the district page or school page
- [ ] organization (school or district) name
- [ ] contact information/e-mail address(es)
- [ ] information crediting any graphics used on the site
- [ ] an information page about the Web site and its creation
- [ ] name(s) of responsible parties (author information/credential page)
- [ ] bibliography or other list of citations

B Each educational Web **page** should include **authority** information such as:
- [ ] title
- [ ] link to the home page
- [ ] navigational tools/menu
- [ ] e-mail address for contacting a staff member or the webmaster
- [ ] copyright statement
- [ ] the page's URL
- [ ] the date the page was created and the date of the most recent update
- [ ] copyright statement

Reproducible from *K–12 Web Pages: Planning & Publishing Excellent School Web Sites* by Debra Kay Logan and Cynthia Beuselinck (Linworth Publishing, Inc., 2002)

FILE NAME WORK SHEET

Project_____

FILE NAME WITH EXTENSION (I.E. .JPG, .GIF, .AU, .WAV, ETC.	IMAGE NAME	PAGE TITLE	DESCRIPTION OF IMAGE AND/OR PAGE WITH USE NOTES

Reproducible from *K–12 Web Pages: Planning & Publishing Excellent School Web Sites* by Debra Kay Logan and Cynthia Beuselinck (Linworth Publishing, Inc., 2002)

IMAGE SOURCE NOTE SHEET

PROJECT

FILE NAME WITH EXTENSION (i.e. .JPG, .GIF, .AU, .WAV, ETC.)	IMAGE NAME	PAGES ON WHICH NOTES WERE USED	SOURCE INCLUDE NAME AND TYPE OF SOURCE. ARTIST, AND LOCATION OF SOURCES (i.e., WEB ADDRESS, LOCATION OF CD)	PERMISSION NOTES INCLUDE RESTRICTIONS & LOCATION OF PERMISSION INFORMATION (i.e., LICENSE AGREEMENT, ONLINE, FOLDER)

Reproducible from *K–12 Web Pages: Planning & Publishing Excellent School Web Sites* by Debra Kay Logan and Cynthia Beuselinck (Linworth Publishing, Inc., 2002)

PREPUBLICATION CHECK SHEET

Date: _____/_____/_____

CHECK PAGES FOR DESIGN FLAWS

- [ ] on different computers
- [ ] variety of screen sizes
- [ ] at different screen resolutions
- [ ] using *Netscape* (older and newer versions)
- [ ] using *Internet Explorer* (older and newer versions)
- [ ] using any other available browsers

USE TOOLS TO EVALUATE SITE FOR ACCESSIBILITY

- [ ] Bobby <http://www.cast.org/bobby/>
- [ ] Wave <http://www.temple.edu/inst_disabilities/piat/wave/>

CHECK PAGES FOR INCONSISTENCIES IN:

- [ ] use of graphics
- [ ] positioning of contents
- [ ] use of color

CHECK ALL LINKS

- [ ] Do they work?
- [ ] Do they link to the correct site?

PROOFREAD, PROOFREAD, & PROOFREAD—PRINT PAGES AND DOUBLE-CHECK

Spelling: [ ] first time   [ ] second time

Grammar: [ ] first time   [ ] second time

Note: Use Web Site Evaluation Form to complete the evaluation process.

PROMOTION CHECK SHEET

Date: _____ / _____ / _____

PROMOTION PLANS

A In the **building** and **district**

District community relations contact person _____

   1. Newsletters _____

     Contact person _____

   2. Letters _____

   3. Public announcements (at special events) _____

   4. In-service training _____

     Staff development contact person _____

   5. Bulletin boards _____

   6. Bookmarks _____

   7. Business cards _____

   8. "Grand opening" events _____

   9. Other _____

     Contact person _____

B In the **community**

District community relations contact person _____

   1. Newsletters _____

     Contact person _____

   2. Newspapers _____

     Newspaper education reporter _____

   3. Radio _____

     Contact person _____

   4. Television _____

     Contact person _____

   5. Letters _____

   6. Public announcements (at special events) _____

Reproducible from *K–12 Web Pages: Planning & Publishing Excellent School Web Sites* by Debra Kay Logan and Cynthia Beuselinck (Linworth Publishing, Inc., 2002)

PROMOTION CHECK SHEET continued

7. In-service training_____

   staff development contact person _____

8. Bookmarks _____

9. Pens, pencils, or other promotional items printed with site address _____

   _____

10. Business cards _____

11. Links from other community sites _____

   ◼ send e-mails notifying intention to link

   ◼ invite to link back

12. "Grand opening" events _____

13. Workshops for:

   Parents _____

   Children _____

   Community members _____

   Adult education coordinator _____

14. Other educators _____

15. Other _____

   contact person _____

C On the **Web**

1. Submission to search engines/tools _____

   ◼ include META tags with keywords and brief description of the site

   ◼ follow instructions for submitting Web sites to search tools

   ◼ use Web engine submission service for submitting site to numerous engines (these resources usually cost money)

2. Notify online educational resource and directory sites

   ◼ look for submission instructions on educational resource sites

   ◼ submit site to school directory Web sites

3. ◼ send e-mails notifying intention to link with invitation to link back

4. Other _____

EVALUATION PLANNING SHEET

Date: _____ / _____ / _____

TYPES OF EVALUATION

- ☐ Traditional Web site evaluation forms _____
- ☐ Survey _____
- ☐ Interviews _____
- ☐ Tracking software _____
- ☐ Observations _____
- ☐ Statistics _____
- ☐ Tracking information _____

TOPICS FOR QUESTIONS

Statistics _____

_____

Usability _____

_____

Accessibility _____

_____

Content effectiveness _____

_____

Appeal _____

_____

Frustrations _____

_____

Weaknesses _____

_____

Strengths _____

_____

Other comments/suggestions _____

_____

Reproducible from *K–12 Web Pages: Planning & Publishing Excellent School Web Sites* by Debra Kay Logan and Cynthia Beuselinck (Linworth Publishing, Inc., 2002)

WEB SITE EVALUATION FORM

Site Name_____ Date: ____/____/____

CRITERIA	UNACCEPTABLE	POOR	GOOD	EXCELLENT
CONTENT:				
Original				
Relevant				
Accurate				
Complete				
Unbiased/objective				
Clear				
Current				
Unique				
Links				
Meaningful graphics				
Appeal				
Commercial content does not interfere with information				
AUTHORITY:				
Site signed				
Author's credentials provided				
Information and credentials verifiable				
Sources credited				
Sponsoring organization identified (if appropriate)				
Contact information given				
AUDIENCE APPROPRIATENESS:				
Accessibility				
Readability				
Concept load				
FORMAT:				
Usable				
Download time				
Ease of navigation				
Searchable				
Functional/usable				
Spelling & grammar correct				
Help provided				
Aesthetically appealing				
COMPLIANT WITH DISTRICT POLICIES:				
Personal information and images				
Copyright restrictions				
Required graphics, links, and so forth				
Headers/footers				
Acceptable file types				
Other				
Other				

Reproducible from *K–12 Web Pages: Planning & Publishing Excellent School Web Sites* by Debra Kay Logan and Cynthia Beuselinck (Linworth Publishing, Inc., 2002)

MAINTENANCE CHECK SHEET

Date: ____/____/____

REVIEW SCHEDULE

Monthly Review Date _____

Annual Review Date _____

CHECK ALL LINKS

Schedule _____

REMOVAL/RELOCATION OF PAGES

Retention & review schedule

Monthly review date _____

Annual review date _____

Customized 404 page   ☐ Yes   ☐ No

Reference pages for relocations   ☐ Yes   ☐ No

Length of time to keep reference pages in place

_____

PLAN FOR DISPOSITION OF REMOVED PAGES

Archive online _____

Archive print or digital copy _____

Reproducible from *K–12 Web Pages: Planning & Publishing Excellent School Web Sites* by Debra Kay Logan and Cynthia Beuselinck (Linworth Publishing, Inc., 2002)

Appendix 2:
Where to Go for Additional Help and Resources

General Web Builder Resource Sites

Software Archives

Software and Hardware Reviews

Organizations and Help for Web Builders

Scripts

Graphics & Color

Validation Tools

Log Analysis Programs and Services

Add-Ons

General Collections

Communications

Other Tools

School Site Awards For Inspiration and Encouragement

▶ GENERAL WEB BUILDER RESOURCE SITES

C/Net Builder.com—Web Building
<http://www.builder.com/>
Here is a comprehensive site dedicated to the issues of Web building. It includes links to products, services, tutorials, newsletters, and many other relevant online resources.

HTML Goodies
<http://www.htmlgoodies.com/>
This collection has at least 100 online tutorials for learning HTML.

Joe Expert
<http://www.joeexpert.com/>
This comprehensive Web development search vortal provides access to tutorials and information for Web authors and developers.

Webmonkey
<http://hotwired.lycos.com/webmonkey/>
Resources and tutorials specifically for Web developers are available here.

Webtools
<http://www.webtools.com/>
Devoted to web development, this searchable site contains articles, tutorials, and software.

▶ SOFTWARE ARCHIVES

C|Net Shareware Archive
<http://shareware.cnet.com/>
C|Net keeps a large archive of shareware for all platforms.

Dave Central
<http://www.davecentral.com/>
This site is a frequently updated software archive for Windows and Linux operating systems.

Simply the Best Shareware
<http://www.simplythebest.net/webutilities.html>
A variety of shareware Web utilities are available from this collection.

Tucows
<http://www.tucows.com/>
Tucows is a well-known software archive for all platforms.

ZDNet Downloads
<http://www.zdnet.com/downloads/>
Search this archive of software from ZD, which includes free downloads and other resources.

⊳ SOFTWARE AND HARDWARE REVIEWS

IT Reviews
<http://www.itreviews.co.uk/>
This collection of reviews of current hardware, software, and computer games is written by professional journalists.

Review Booth
<http://www.reviewbooth.com/>
Here is a searchable database of software and hardware reviews that is updated weekly.

ZD Net Reviews
<http://www.zdnet.com/products/>
Another searchable collection of reviews on hardware, software, and other computer products is found on this ZD site.

⊳ ORGANIZATIONS AND HELP FOR WEB BUILDERS

Classroom Connect's Connected Teacher E-mail List
<http://listserv.classroom.com/archives/crc.html>
From Classroom Connect, this e-mail list allows teachers to share Internet-related information specific to K–12 education.

HTML Writer's Guild
<http://www.hwg.org/>
The official site of the HTML Writer's Guild, an international organization of Web authors, provides "resources, support, representation, and education for Web authors at all skill levels."

International Webmasters Association
<http://www.iwanet.org/>
This is a nonprofit international association for Web professionals.

International Association of Webmasters and Designers
<http://www.iawmd.com/main.shtml>
Similar to the International Webmasters Association, IAWMD is an international association of webmasters and designers dedicated to providing education, awareness, and networking for those working on and with the Web.

SchoolWebs: School Web Site Managements
<http://groups.yahoo.com/group/schoolwebs/>
SchoolWebs "addresses issues specific to K–12 website development and management" "through "shared experiences, resources, concerns, questions, and supportive critiques from school webmasters."

TechCoordinator Forum
<http://groups.yahoo.com/group/TechCoordinator/>
The mission of this discussion forum is "to promote issues important to Technology Coordinators of educational institutions (schools, libraries and museums)."

WebQuest Forum

<http://groups.yahoo.com/group/webquest/>

"This is a forum for sharing ideas, insights, problems and solutions for those using the WebQuest model in their teaching."

▶ SCRIPTS

Free Code

<http://www.freecode.com/>

The Free Code site has many free snippets of code and scripts for Unix and Windows, many of which are for use with Web sites.

GetScripts

<http://www.scripts.com/index.html>

GetScripts is another collection of free scripts and snippets of code for creating counters, banners, clocks, and much more.

The JavaScript Source

<http://javascript.internet.com/toc.html>

This site is a cut-and-paste library of free JavaScript code.

JavaScript World

<http://www.jsworld.com/>

JavaScript World is a reference site that also offers plenty of sample code.

Mighty Mouseover Machine

<http://www.builder.com/Programming/Kahn/012898/>

The Mighty Mouseover Machine is an online tool for automatically creating rollover effects. Complete a form to generate the code, then copy and paste the code into local Web page files.

▶ GRAPHICS & COLOR

2Learn: Communications Technology Graphics

<http://www.2learn.ca/comtech/TechSiteGraph.html>

Developed by the Telus 2Learn project, this collection of clip art and tips on using graphics is especially for educators.

GifWorks: Free Online eTools

<http://www.gifworks.com>

This image editor runs online. After modifying, download and save the images locally.

JavaScript Color Cube

<http://www.shorewalker.com/channel/colorcube.html>

This site provides a dynamic display of colors and their corresponding hex values that change as the mouse moves over each color.

Javazoom TYPO

<http://javazoom.hypermart.net/services/typo/jztypo.html>

At Javazoom, the TYPO font builder will automatically create customized fonts based on user input through a form. The font becomes a transparent gif, which is then saved locally.

Open Directory—Computers: Graphics: Web: Tutorials

<http://dmoz.org/Computers/Graphics/WebGraphics/Tutorials/>

The Open Directory Project provides directories of evaluated sites on various topics. This collection consists of tutorials for working with graphics.

Simply the Best Graphics Compression Shareware

<http://www.simplythebest.net/compress.html>

This collection of tools is for doing graphics compression.

▶ VALIDATION TOOLS

Validation Tools

<http://www.webdesign.about.com/compute/webdesign/cs/validationtools/>

As the name suggests, this site is a collection of Web site validation tools and software from about.com.

W3C Link Checker

<http://www.w3.org/2000/07/checklink>

The World Wide Web Consortium is the standards body for the Web. This section of its site provides a link-checking tool that can be downloaded and run locally or run across the Web.

Website Garage

<http://websitegarage.netscape.com/>

From Netscape Communications, this online validation tool will check links, browser compatibility, download times, and much more.

Xenu's Link Sleuth

<http:/home.snafu.de/tilman/xenulink.html>

Xenu is a fast, free, link-checking software that is downloaded and run from a local workstation. It checks internal and external links, allows for some customization, and generates easy-to-understand reports in HTML format.

▶ LOG ANALYSIS PROGRAMS AND SERVICES

SEVENtwentyfour

<http://www.seventwentyfour.com/>

SEVENtwentyfour is an online link analysis service that is available by paid subscription and runs a variety of specialized statistics and reports on Web sites. Pricing varies by the size of the site and the services selected.

The Webalizer

<http://www.mrunix.net/webalizer/index.html>

This log analysis tool is free, but must be downloaded and installed on the server to run.

WebLog
<http://awsd.com/scripts/weblog/>

Provided by WebScripts, WebLog is a log analysis software that is downloaded and installed on a local server. It generates reports showing visitor traffic, browsers used, referring pages, search terms used, and many other statistical items.

Webtrends
<http://webtrends.com>

Webtrends is a well-known and commonly used log analysis software in industry. It is highly customizable with many charts and options for manipulating and reporting log data. It must be purchased for installation on a local server.

⊳ ADD-ONS

General Collections

Bravenet Web Services
<http://www.bravenet.com/>

Registration is required to use these tools, but Bravenet provides a large collection of free goodies, including counters, polls, guest books, and more. Some are snippets of code that can be copied to a local site; others run from the Bravenet server.

Twest Applications
<http://www.twest.de/index_en.php>

Twest is an application service provider that has a number of free services, including polls, calendars, quizzes, or a guest book.

Communications

BoardHost
<http://www.boardhost.com>

This site allows registrants to customize and use free message boards.

NiceNet's Internet Classroom Assistant
<http://www.nicenet.org/>

Designed especially for educational use, NiceNet offers a number of free services to simulate an online classroom.

Topica
<http://www.topica.com/index.html>

Topica has a large collection of discussion groups and lists, but it also allows visitors to create their own discussion groups and lists.

Yahoo Groups
<http://groups.yahoo.com/>

Like Topica, Yahoo also allows users to create discussion forums and chats free of charge.

UltraBoard

<http://www.ub2k.com/>

UltraBoard is highly customizable and has no advertising, but it requires downloading and local installation.

▶ OTHER TOOLS

Anaconda Foundation

<http://www.anaconda.net/ap_famazondemo.shtml>

Using this tool, webmasters can increase revenue from Amazon by dynamically generating lists of books for individual purchase.

Calendars Net

<http://www.calendars.net/>

This site allows visitors to create a dynamic online calendar. Calendars.net hosts the calendar; it is not saved locally.

Freedback

<http://freedback.com/>

Freedback provides customizable interactive forms that do not need any cgi scripting installed on the local server.

Hot Potatoes

<http://web.uvic.ca/hrd/halfbaked/>

Hot Potatoes is a software for creating online quizzes. It is free to educational institutions, providing they make the quizzes available online at no cost.

Magportal

<http://www.magportal.com/help/free_feeds/what_is.html>

This site provides live feed of magazine article headlines available by free subscription to webmasters. Select the magazines by topic so the feed is relevant to the site.

Moreover

<http://w.moreover.com/site/products/webmaster/index.html>

Moreover provides a free, customizable, live news feed that can easily be added to a Web site.

Super Calendar

<http://www.supercalendar.com/>

Here is another site for creating a free, dynamic events calendar that can be added to any Web site without additional HTML programming.

▶ SCHOOL SITE AWARDS—FOR INSPIRATION AND ENCOURAGEMENT

Becta Awards

<http://www.becta.org.uk/schools/websiteawards/index.html>

The British Educational Communications and Technology Agency give out the Becta Awards for school Web sites in the U.K.

Canada SchoolNet
<http://www.schoolnet.ca/builders/e/>
The School Web Site Builder Awards is awarded weekly, monthly, and annually to Canadian Schools through Canada SchoolNet.

Education World
<http://www.education-world.com/cool_school/>
Education World offers the Cool School of the Week Award for sites developed by students.

EduNet Choice
<http://www.edunetconnect.com/choiceaw.html>
From EduNet, this award is given to Web sites for valuable educational content.

Gigglepotz Site of the Week
<http://www.gigglepotz.com/schools.htm>
Gigglepotz features the Cool School Award, which is presented weekly to school Web sites around the world.

Innovative Teaching Concepts
<http://www.twoteach.com/AwardofExcellence.htm>
Innovative Teaching Concepts offers two awards. One is an award of excellence given to school Web sites, and the second is for sites created by students.

Learning Alive
<http://www.learningalive.co.uk/>
Previously EduWeb, Learning Alive offers awards of the week to primary and secondary school Web sites.

School Library Journal
<http://www.slj.com/articles/siteofthemonth/sotmindex.asp>
Each month, School Library Journal selects a school library site of the month.

School World Site of the Month Award
<http://www.schoolworld.asn.au/swaward/>
These school Web site awards are open only to members of School World.

USA Today Best Bets
<http://www.edgate.com/usatoday/best_bets/> (archive of winners)
<http://www.edgate.com/educate/bet.html> (submission form)
USA Today Best Bets school Web site awards are given weekly by staff from USA Today Education Online.

Glossary

ABSOLUTE LINK   link that uses the complete URL/Web address, including the leading http://.

ACCESSIBILITY   making Web content usable by people with disabilities.

AUTHORING TOOL   specialized software used to create Web pages that generates HTML code automatically.

ADVERTISING BANNER   graphic that appears on Web pages that contain advertisements. Often the ads "rotate" or change automatically.

ALT ATTRIBUTE (also ALT tag)   using an ALT tag/attribute is a way of offering descriptive text as an alternative to an image or link.

ARCHIVE   collection of documents that is saved for historical or legal purposes. Can also mean the act of saving the documents.

AUDIO CLIP   short file containing recorded audio (sounds, music, voice).

BANDWIDTH   measures amount and speed of data transmitted through a connection during a specific amount of time.

BIT   one electric pulse that is "understood by computers." Bits are on or off.

BROWSER   software program that enables the viewing of World Wide Web resources on computers. *Internet Explorer* and *Netscape Communicator* are examples of browsers.

CASCADING STYLE SHEETS (CSS)   programming method that allows the Web author to set specific styles and formats in HTML documents that can be applied automatically to multiple Web pages. CSS give Web creators greater control over the "look" of Web pages.

CGI (COMMON GATEWAY INTERFACE) SCRIPT   script written in another programming language, such as PERL or C++, that can be used to program elements such as passwords, the submission of some types of forms, and counters.

CELL (TABLE)   unit in a table in which data or copy is entered.

COMPRESSION TOOLS   programs that reduce the size of files.

COMPUTER ETHICS   standards of conduct pertaining to the use of computers.

CONNECTIVITY   various devices that link a network together.

CSS   see **CASCADING STYLE SHEETS**

DIRECTORY   see **FOLDER**

DISCLAIMER   statement made by an organization noting that it is not responsible for certain content or ideas.

DHTML   Dynamic HTML; Web pages that are generated as they are requested as opposed to being coded as static HTML documents (i.e., a list of search results).

DIGITIZED IMAGE   images that have been converted into an electronic format through a graphics tablet or by scanning.

DNS see **DOMAIN NAME SYSTEM**

DNS SERVER servers located around the world that keep databases of DNS (Domain Name System) entries. Each time someone requests a domain by name (by typing in www.domain-name.com), the request goes to a DNS server somewhere in the world to be resolved to the number that designates the specific computer on which the information is located.

DOMAIN the unique and registered name/address of a Web site.

DOMAIN NAME SYSTEM method of connecting domain names with specific computers on the Internet. Computers are addressed by numbers, which are connected to recognizable names (such as apple.com) by means of the Domain Name System.

DOWNLOAD to electronically move information in the form of a file from a distant/remote computer to a local computer.

DOWNLOAD TIME the length of time it takes for a file to get from a remote computer to your computer.

EXECUTABLE program file designed to run independently (usually has an .exe extension).

EXTENSION the three-or-four letter ending after the dot in a file name that defines the type of file (.doc is a Word document, .txt is a text document, .htm or .html is a Web page document, .gif is a type of graphic file, and so forth). Extensions are sometimes not visible in the file name on personal computers; changes can be made in the settings so the extensions do not appear when file names are listed.

FTP see **FILE TRANSFER PROTOCOL**

FILE EXTENSION the three- or four-characters after the dot at the end of a file name that designate the file type being used (.doc for a Word document, .htm or .html for a Web page).

FILE SIZE the size of an individual file in bytes, not dimensions.

FILE TYPE exactly what kind of file, often categorized by the file extension.

FILE TRANSFER PROTOCOL protocol that enables the movement of information between distant computers.

FLASH animation software that is used to create Web page multimedia.

FOLDER On Macintosh and Windows systems, users can create folders that hold common files together in a collection. On other operating systems, folders are sometimes referred to as directories.

FOOTER information consistently found at the bottom/foot of every Web site page. Footers frequently include author, update, copyright, and contact information.

FORM HANDLER scripts that direct the processing of a Web-based form.

FONT FAMILY set of fonts that have common stroke widths and characteristics.

FONT set of typeface characters.

404 ERROR PAGE indicates that a Web page/file is not found.

FRAMES   stationary portion of a Web site used to divide browser windows into two or more distinct scrollable areas.

GIF (GRAPHICS INTERCHANGE FORMAT)   type of image format commonly used for line drawings or for images with few or single colors on the Web.

HEADER   information that consistently appears at the top or head of each Web page on a Web site. Could include titles, text, or images.

HEXADECIMAL CODE   base-16 mathematical calculation used to convert RGB (red, green, blue) color values into a set of 6 alphanumeric characters so they can be used in HTML. Hexadecimal color codes designate a specific color from the millions of colors available in the spectrum.

HEXADECIMAL COLOR CHART   color chart that includes the RGB (red, green, blue) colors that have been translated into hexadecimal code. Of the 256 colors found on the Hexadecimal Color Chart, 216 are considered Web safe (see **WEB SAFE COLORS**).

HIERARCHICAL STRUCTURE   arrangement of Web pages in which users are intended to start at the top level of pages and move down through the pages.

HIT COUNTER   program or service that tracks the number of times a page has been accessed or "hit." Some hit counters track hits only to a page while others count each file that is loaded as a hit (so loading a page with five graphics creates six hits instead of one).

HOME PAGE   the opening page of a series of connected pages on the WWW (World Wide Web). A collection of pages as a unit is called a Web site.

HOST   computer that is the source of information shared on a network. Also refers to the organization that provides the storage space for a Web site.

HOST NAME   the location of the host where Web pages are to be uploaded; required to make a connection to a specific computer on the Internet.

HTML   see **HYPERTEXT MARKUP LANGUAGE**

HYPERTEXT   text, usually highlighted by color or underlined, that creates a link to other resources on the Internet or within a Web page or Web site. Graphics can be hyperlinks also.

HYPERTEXT MARKUP LANGUAGE   the text-based code that is translated by browser software and enables Web pages to contain formatted text, graphics, video, hyperlinks, sounds, and so forth.

HYPERLINK   the graphic or hypertext that forms the connection between two documents on the Internet or an Intranet.

ISP   see **INTERNET SERVICE PROVIDER**

IMAGE MAP   graphic that has sections of the image hyperlinked to other documents or pages.

INTERCONNECTED STRUCTURE   arrangement of Web pages in which pages are all connected to each other, allowing users to move freely within the Web site.

INTERNET   world wide network of computers that connect by using similar protocols. This system provides access to databases, e-mail, discussion and news groups, programs and other computer files, and other forms of information and communication.

INTERNET EXPLORER   Web browser software created by Microsoft Corporation.

INTERNET SERVICE PROVIDER (ISP)   business or organization that provides access to the Internet.

INTRANET   network of computers that can be accessed only by users within an organization.

JAVA   programming language used to create programs that run on all platforms.

JAVASCRIPT   programmed scripts that cause specified actions. Drop-down menus and scrolling text are often created using JavaScript.

JPEG OR JPG (JOINT PHOTOGRAPHIC EXPERT GROUP)   type of image format commonly used for photographs, art, and other types of full-color, continuous tone images on the Web.

LINEAR STRUCTURE   arrangement of pages that moves users through a Web site step by step in a prescribed "1, 2, 3" type order.

LINK   WWW connection from one location to another. Links can be to other resources on the Internet or within a Web page or a Web site.

LINK CHECKER   program or service that checks a Web site for broken or relocated hyperlinks.

LINK ROT   broken hyperlinks on a Web site.

LINUX   popular version of Unix available for free; paid versions come with technical support and training.

LISTSERV   automatic message services that deliver e-mail to subscribers.

MACINTOSH OS   the operating system on Macintosh computers. The Macintosh OS has a graphical user interface (GUI).

MAINTENANCE TOOL   software or service that performs maintenance checks on the functionality of a Web site, such as spelling and syntax.

MENU   list of links to a Web site's other pages found on each page of the site. A menu is a navigation tool.

META TAG   underlying bit of code that can be used to identify information about the Web site, such as keywords, the title, a description, and the author.

MULTIMEDIA   combines the use of formats such as text, images, videos, and sound.

NAMING CONVENTION   a standard method of naming files and folders.

NAVIGATION   how users move through the pages and layers of a Web site.

NAVIGATION TOOLS   set of menus or buttons that is linked to different sections of a Web site.

NETSCAPE   Web browser software created by Netscape Communications Corporation, which is now owned by AOL.

NETWORK   system of computers that are all connected and share resources, files, and programs.

NEWBIE   person who is new to the Web or to a group on the Internet.

NEWSGROUP electronic form of bulletin board where messages are left for others to read. Typical messages are questions and information. Must have a newsreader on a browser to participate in a newsgroup.

ONLINE DIRECTORY lists of addresses, phone numbers, names, and so forth (like a phone book) that are accessible through the Internet.

ONLINE MAP CREATION TOOL Web site that dynamically generates maps based on addresses or directions input by the user.

OPERA Web browser software created by Opera Software of Norway.

ORPHAN PAGE page that does not have links to its Web site's home page or to the rest of the Web site.

PAGE LAYOUT arrangement of elements (banners, images, buttons, and so forth) on a Web page.

PATH NAME route to a specific file (see **ABSOLUTE LINK** and **RELATIVE LINK**).

PIXEL elements of pictures that are turned off or on to create/display images. Pixels can range in capacity from 1-bit pixels capable of showing 2 colors to 24-bit pixels that can display 65,536 colors.

PLATFORM hardware or operating system being used (Macintosh, Windows, Unix, and so forth).

PLUG-INS additional pieces of software that are used with browsers to permit the utilization of multimedia files on the Web. Some plug-ins need to be downloaded and installed. Other plug-ins are installed with browser software.

PNG (PORTABLE NETWORK GRAPHIC) relatively newer type of image format created for use on the Web. PNGs are highly compressed images that do not lose data when saved. PNGs are cross platform.

PORTAL special type of Web site that offers multiple services from one site, such as hosting, news, e-mail, search tools, directories, and links to selected sites. Portals that cater to a specific market (such as education) are called Vertical Portals, or Vortals.

PROPRIETARY format or program that is nonstandard or produces nonstandard results.

PUBLISHING GUIDELINES suggestions and recommendations that direct the authoring and management of Web pages.

PUBLISHING POLICIES regulations that must be followed in the authoring and management of Web pages.

PUSH PAGE automatically moves user to another Web page. Commonly found when Web sites have been moved.

RGB stands for red, green, and blue. These three colors are emitted by monitors to display all images/visuals.

REFERENCE PAGES refers users to the new location of a page or Web site that has been moved.

RELATIVE LINK   link that uses only part of a URL/Web address to request pages or files on the same server or within the same Web site.

RETENTION PERIOD   specified length of time before documents are removed or relocated.

REVERSE DIRECTORY   type of directory that looks up information using only an address or phone number rather than searching by name.

SCRIPT   special purpose programs that are designed to work as additions to the HTML code in Web pages.

SEARCH ENGINE   search tool that allows visitors to type in specific terms for which the tool will search.

SEARCH TOOL   generic term that refers to all the categories of search technologies available on the Web. Includes directories, catalogs, and search engines.

SERVER   computer or program that provides access to other computers or systems.

SERVER ADMINISTRATOR   person who manages the server.

SITE STRUCTURE   how pages on a Web site are arranged and connected to each other.

SPACE ALLOCATION   amount of storage given for folders or files on the server.

SPECIAL CHARACTERS   characters that are not letters or numbers, such as $, %, &, +, @, #. File names for the Web cannot contain the following special characters: /, \, <, >," |, ;

SPLASH PAGE   opening page that usually has a large image and little else.

STATISTICS REPORTING TOOLS   program or service that keeps track of data about Web site usage.

SYNTAX   rules for formulating statements within a programming language; exactly how words and symbols must be put together so the programming is correct and will work.

SYNTAX CHECKER   program or service that checks the programming code of Web pages or scripts.

TABLE   rows of cells. Originally tables were used for tabular information. Now they are commonly used for page layout.

TEMPLATE   pre-designed document that provides a common format or style on which other documents are based.

THUMBNAIL   smaller, lower-resolution version of an image.

UNIX   widely used operating system on the Internet available in many versions and for different platforms. A graphical user interface is now available for Unix.

UPLOAD   to electronically move a file from a local computer to a distant/remote computer.

URL   stands for Universal Resource Locator or Uniform Resource Locator. It means Web address.

VORTAL   see **PORTAL**

WYSIWYG   acronym for "what you see is what you get." Refers to the Web creator being able to work with creating and manipulating the elements of the page graphically, rather than working in code. Used with Web authoring software.

WEB BROWSER   see **BROWSER**

WEB SAFE COLORS   the 216 colors that can be found on Macintosh and PC Systems. Those 216 colors are among the 256 RGB (red, green, blue) colors. Some browsers do not make provisions for all 256 RGB colors. If a color is outside of the Web safe palette, the browser "chooses" a replacement color.

WEB STRUCTURE see **INTERCONNECTED STRUCTURE**

WHITE SPACE   amount of blank space used to enhance design and readability of a document.

WINDOWS   the most widely used operating system on personal computers. Windows OS has a graphical user interface (GUI).

WORLD WIDE WEB (WWW)   The part of the Internet that allows documents with graphics, text, videos, and sounds to link/connect to other resources through the Internet using Hyperlinks.

Works Cited and Selected Recommended Resources List

This bibliography lists resources that contributed to the intellectual content of the book. Some of the items listed have been cited in the book and others were read and used by authors during their research process. The latter resources are listed here for further reading and research. Throughout the book the reader will find helpful tools listed in resource boxes. Tools like color pallets and link checkers are not listed in this *Works Cited and Selected Recommended Resources List*. The list is intended to help readers expand their knowledge of the topics covered in this book and to acknowledge sources that have been directly quoted.

Arbor Heights Elementary School. The Arbor Heights www site. 2 October 2001
     <http://www.halcyon.com/arborhts/history.html>.

Bellingham Public Schools. *Designing School Home Pages*. 13 February 2001.
   <http://www.bham.wednet.edu/homepage.htm>.

Bellingham Public Schools. *Web Publishing Rules*. 1996. 13 June 2001
   <http://www.bham.wednet.edu/copyrule.htm>.

Benson, Allen C., and Linda M. Fodemski. *Connecting Kids and the Internet: A Handbook for Librarians, Teachers, and Parents Second Edition.* Neal-Schuman Publishers, Inc., 1999.

Bowen, Candace Perkins. "What Are Your Students Publishing on the Web?"
   The School Administrator Web Edition, April 1998. 9 February 2001
   <http://www.aasa.org/publications/sa/1998_04/Perkins-Bowen.htm>.

Branigan, Cara. "FBI Urges Schools to Ban Web-site Student Photos, but Not All Educators Agree." *eSchool News*, July 24, 2000. 18 February 2001
   <http://www.eshcoolnews.com/showstory.cfm?ArticleID=1342>.

Brinson, Dianne, and Mark F. Radcliffe. *An Intellectual Property Law Primer for Multimedia and Web Developers.* 1996. 15 February 2001
   <http://www.eff.org/pub/CAF/law/ip-primer>.

Brunwelheide, Janis H. *The Copyright Primer for Librarians and Educators Second Edition.* American Library Association and National Education Association, 1995.

Calgary Board of Education. *Acceptable Posting Practice.* 1997.
   <http://www.cbe.ab.ca/intranet2/app.htm>.

Canadian Intellectual Property Office. *Frequently Asked Questions: Copyright.* 2000.
   16 February 2001 <http://strategis.ic.gc.ca/sc_mrksv/cipo/help/faq_cp-e.html>.

Carroll, Lewis. *Alice's Adventures in Wonderland and Through the Looking Glass.* Signet Classic, 2000.

Center for Advanced Technologies in Education. *Legal and Ethical Issues Related to the Use of the Internet in K–12 Schools.* 11 February 2001 <http://206.98.102.208/documents/leicontent.html>.

Cerdon College. *Publication of Student Work on the Internet.* 1998. 17 June 2001 <http://www.schools.ash.org.au/cerdon/policies/interpol.htm>.

Champelli, Lisa, and Howard Rosenbaum. *WebMaster.* Neal-Schuman Publishers, Inc., 1997.

Clarke, Arthur C. *The Lost Worlds of 2001.* Sidgwick & Jackson, 1976.

Cole, Linda. "Purloining and Pilfering." *The Web Developer's Virtual Library.* 29 January 2001 <http://www.stars.com/Graphics/Theft/>.

Cupertino Union School District. *World Wide Web Guidelines.* 13 June 2001 <http://www.cupertino.k12.ca.us/Do.www/W3guide.html>.

Dahl, Roald. *Charlie and the Chocolate Factory.* Knopf, 1964.

Dale, Jack. Personal interview. 10 February 2001.

Davis School District. *Davis School District Internet/Intranet Publishing Guidelines.* 2000. 17 June 2001 <http://www.davis.k12.ut.us/websters/iipguide.htm>.

Dennis-Yarmouth Regional School District. *Suggested Guidelines for School, Department and Classroom Web Pages.* 13 June 2001 <http://www.dy-regional.k12.ma.us/pdf/schoolwebpages.pdf>.

Dryden, John. *Alexander's Feast, or the Power of Music; An Ode in Honour of St. Cecilia's Day 1697.* September Press, 1985.

Eggleston. T. S. *What Every Webmaster Needs to Know About Copyright.* 29 January 2001 <http://pw1.netcom.com/%7Enuance/crlaw.html>.

Fairbanks North Star Borough School District. *Web Publishing Standards and Guidelines.* 13 June 2001 <http://www.northstar.k12.ak.us/guides/standards.html>.

Field, Thomas G. Jr. *Copyright for Computer Authors*, 2 September 2000. 29 January 2001 < http://www.fplc.edu/tfield/cOpySof.htm>.

Field,Thomas G. Jr, *Copyright on the Internet.* 2 September 2000. 29 January 2001 <http://www.fplc.edu/tfield/cOpyNet.htm>.

Flanders, Vincent, and Michael Willis. *Web Pages That Suck: Learn Good Design by Looking at Bad Design.* Sybex, 1996.

Gasaway, Laura N. *Copyright Law in the Digital Age: Course Materials* (workshop handbook). University of North Carolina, 2000.

Germantown Academy. *Ganet Acceptable Publication Policy*. 1997. 17 June 2001
    <http://www.germantownacademy.com/Oursite/APP.htm>.

Gillespie, Joe, and Sarah R. Yoffa. *High Five Feature Article*. 29 January 2001
    < http://www.wpdfd.com/H5/997.htm>.

Global Schoolhouse. 3. To Publish Names, Photos, and E-mail addresses. 11 February 2000.
    <http://gsh.lightspan.com/web/webproj/define/protect/pubnames.html>
    (4 October 2001)

Grand Erie District School Board. *Web Publishing Guidelines*. 1999.
    <http://www.whs.on.ca/webpublishingdoc.doc>.

Guidelines for Educational Use of Copyrighted Materials. Ed. Peggy Hoon. Pullman:
    Washington State University Press, 1997.

Hillsboro School District. *Hillsboro School District Web Publishing Guidelines*. 2001. 17 June 2001
    <http://www.hsd.k12.or.us/district/technology/webpublish.htm>.

Hixson, Susan, and Kathleen Schrock. *Beginner's Handbook: Developing Web Pages for
    School and Classroom*. Teacher Created Materials, Inc., 1998.

Holzschlag, Molly E. *Using HTML 4.0 Sixth Edition*. Que Corporation, 2000.

*Implementing and Managing Web Site Development in Education: Best Practices for Alberta
    School Jurisdictions*. Alberta: Alberta Education, 1999. 15 September 1999
    <http://www.learning.gov.ab.ca/technology/bestpractices/pdf/websitedevelopment.pdf>.

Johnson, Doug. "Teacher Web Pages That Build Parent Partnerships." *Multimedia Schools*,
    September 2000. 29 January 2001
    <http://www.infotoday.com/MMSchools/sep00/johnson.htm> .

Jordan, Michael. *I Can't Accept Not Trying: Michael Jordan on the Pursuit of Excellence*.
    HarperSanFrancisco, 1994.

Joseph, Linda C. *Cyberbee: Web Construction*. 29 January 2001
    <http://www.cyberbee.com/schoolpage/school.html>.

Junion-Metz, Gail, and Brad Stephens. *Creating a Power Web Site: HTML, Tables, Imagemaps,
    Frames, and Forms*. Neal-Schuman Publishers, Inc., 1998.

Kaiser, Jean. *About.Com Color in Web Design*. 2001. 13 June 2001
    <http://webdesign.about.com/compute/webdesign/library/weekly/aa082399.htm>.

Kent, Peter. *Poor Richard's Web Site: Geek-Free Commonsense Advice on Building a Low Cost
    Web Site Second Edition*. Top Floor Publishing, Inc., 2000.

Kim, Leo. *Streamline Your Code*. C|Net, 1998. 18 February 2001
    < http://www.builder.com/Authoring/HtmlDiet/index.html?bb>.

Kovacs, Diane. *Building Electronic Library Collections: The Essential Guide to Selection, Criteria and Core Subject Collections.* Neal-Schuman, 2000.

Kovacs, Diane, and Michael Kovacs. *The Cybrarian's Guide to Developing Successful Internet Programs and Services.* Neal-Schuman Publishers, Inc., 1997.

Lakeville Area Public Schools. *District Web Policy.* 2000. 17 June 2001 <http://www.isd194.k12.mn.us/webpoly.htm>.

Ludwig, Susan F. "Working with Parents." *Teaching PreK–8,* October 1999. 2 October 2000. *Mastefile Premier, EBSCO.* #2291843.

Lutzker, Arnold P., et. al. *The Digital Millennium Copyright Act: Highlights of New Copyright Provision Establishing Limitation of Liability for Online Service Providers Executive Summary.* 18 November 1998. 13 June 2001 <http://www.ala.org/washoff/osp.html>.

Lynch, Patrick J., and Sarah Horton. *Web Style Guide: Basic Design Principles for Creating Web Sites.* Yale University Press, 1999.

Mackay, A. L. *A Dictionary of Scientific Quotations.* 1991. 20 February 2001 [accessed through Xrefer <www.xrefer.com>.

Madison City School. *School Systems and School Web Sites.* Available at <http://www.madisoncity.k12.al.us/Policies/IFBGA.htm>.

Madison Metropolitan School District. *Guidelines and Suggestions for School Web Sites.* May 27, 1999. 13 February, 2001 <http://www.madison.k12.wi.us/hpguides.htm>.

Mankato School District 77. *World Wide Web Page Creation Guidelines.* 1996. 13 June 2001 <http://www.isd77.k12.mn.us/webguide.html>.

McKenzie, Jamie. *FNO Designing School Web Sites to Deliver.* 29 January 2001 <http://fno.org/webdesign.html>.

McKenzie, Jamie. *Home Sweet Home: Creating WWW Pages That Deliver.* 10 February 2001 <http://www.fno.org/homesweet.html>.

McKenzie, Jamie. *Keeping It Legal: Questions Arising out of Web Site Management.* 29 January 2001 <http://www.fno.org/jun96/legal.html>.

Metz, Ray E., and Gail Junion-Metz. *Using the World Wide Web and Creating Home Pages.* Neal-Schuman Publishers, Inc., 1996.

Milbury, Peter. *Making Best Use of the Internet to Enhance Your School Library Program.* Bureau of Education & Research, 2000.

Miller, Elizabeth. *The Internet Resource Directory for K–12 Teachers and Librarians 2000/2001 Edition.* Libraries Unlimited, 2000.

Milne, A. A. *The Complete Tales of Winnie-the-Pooh*. Dutton Children's Books, 1994.

Minneapolis Public Schools District #1. *World Wide Web Page Development Guidelines*. 17 June 2001 <http://www.mpls.k12.mn.us/policies/6415D.html>.

Montgomery County Public Schools. *Policy Statement for the Publishing of Documents on the Internet/World Wide Web*. 17 June 2000 <http://courses.csvt.edu/~cs3604/lib/WorldCodes/AUP.Montgomery.html>.

Morris, Kenneth M. *User's Guide to the Information Age: A Straight-Talking Guide to How Our World Is Connected and How Information Shapes Our Lives*. Lightbulb Press, Inc., 1999.

Mount Carmel Area School District. 2001. *Legal Notices and Trademarks*. 17 June 2001 <http://www.mca.k12.pa.us/legal.html>.

Nielsen, Jakob. *Alertbox: Avoid PDF for On-Screen Reading*. 10 June 2001. 11 June 2001 < http://www.useit.com/alertbox/20010610.html >.

Nielson, Jakob. *Alertbox: Flash 99% Bad*. 29 October 2000. 13 June 2001 <http://www.useit.com/alertbox/20001029.html>.

Nielsen, Jakob. *Alertbox: How Users Read on the Web*. 1 October 1997. 13 June 2001 <http://www.useit.com/alertbox/9710a.html>.

Nielsen, Jakob. *Designing Web Usability*. New Riders Publishing, 2000.

O'Donnell, Pat. *Publishing Student Information Online and Acceptable Use Policies*. 9 February 2001 <http://myschoolonline.com/article/0,1120,36-12551,00.html>.

Oppedahl & Larson Web Law FAQ. 10 August 1999. 29 January 2001 <http://www.patents.com/weblaw.sht>.

Paciello, Michael G. *Web Accessibility for People with Disabilities*. CMP Books, 2000.

Parker, Neil. *Microsoft FrontPage 2000—Level 1*. CCI Learning Solutions, Inc. 2000.

Pope, Alexander. *Essay on Man*. Dover, 1994.

Public Commission of Canada. *Employment Equity Enabling Resources Centre for Persons with Disabilities*. 1 January 2001. 1 October 2001 <http://www.psc-cfp.gc.ca/eepmp-pmpee/program_overview/eeera_2_e.htm>

Rashes, Haran C. "School Liability and the Internet." *School Liability and the Internet: Internet Security and Legal Issues*. 14 February 2001 <http://supportnet.merit.edu/m-intsec/t-dislia/text/intro.html>.

Richmond School Board. *Web Site Content Restrictions and Responsibilities*. 2000. 13 June 2001 <http://www.sd38.bc.ca/WebPolicy/Web_Policy/RSB_Web_Pages05.html>.

Sacred Heart School. *Sacred Heart School Web Site Policy.* 13 June 2001
<http://www.mcraeclan.com/SHS/SHSWebPolicy.htm>.

Santo, Cristine. "Goodbye Bake Sales." *Family PC,* October 1999. 31 January 2001. *Mastefile Premier, EBSCO. #2255764.*

Seydel, Angela. "Fund-raising While You Shop: A Look at Fund-Raising on the Internet." *Multimedia Schools,* September 2000.

Shakespeare, William. *Othello.* Dover, 1996.

Simpson, Carol. *Copyright for Schools: A Practical Guide Third Edition.* Linworth Publishing, Inc., 2001.

Simpson, Carol, and Sharron L. McElmeel. *Internet for Schools: A Practical Guide Third Edition.* Linworth Publishing, Inc., 2000.

Slaton, Joyce. *Shopping for a Better World.* 15 February 2000. February 5, 2001
< http://www.wired.com/news/culture/0,1284,34066,00.html>.

Spring Branch Independent School District. *SBISD Electronic Communication and Data Management Guidelines.* 13 June 2001
<http://www.spring-branch.isd.tenet.edu/admin/tcom/policy/guidelines.htm>.

Talab, R. S. *Commonsense Copyright: A Guide for Educators and Librarian Third Edition.* MacFarland & Co. Inc. Publishing, 1999.

The TechEncyclopedia. CMP Media, 2001. 13 June 2001 <http://www.techweb.com/encyclopedia/home>.

Templeton, Brad. *10 Big Myths About Copyright Explained.* 29 January 2001
< http://www.templetons.com/brad/copymyths.html>.

"To Publish Names, Photos, and Email Addresses." *Building a Collaborative Web Project.* 11 February 2000. 9 February 2001
<http://gsh.lightspan.com/web/webproj/define/protect/pubnames.htm>.

United States Copyright Office. 15 August 2000. 29 January 2001
<http://lcweb.loc.gov/copyright/>.

United States Copyright Office. *Copyright Basics.* 31 January 2000. 16 February 2001
<http://lcweb.loc.gov/copyright/circs/circ01.pdf>.

United States Copyright Office. *Copyright Office Circular 1: Copyright Basics: Who Can Claim Copyright.* December 2000. 15 February 2001
<http://lcweb.loc.gov/copyright/circs/circ1.html#wccc>.

United States Copyright Office. *Copyright Office Circular 66: Copyright Registration for Online Works.* June 1999. 29 January 2001 <http://lcweb.loc.gov/copyright/circs/circ66.pdf>.

University of Wisconsin-Madison. *Accessibility Guidelines for WWW Home Pages.* 2000. <http://www.wisc.edu/wiscinfo/policy/guidelines.html>.

U.S. Department of Justice. "A Guide to Disability Rights Laws." May 2000. 16 February 2001 <http://www.usdoj.gov/crt/ada/cguide.htm#anchor62335>.

Valley Elementary School. *Valley Elementary School Legal Notice.* 1999. 17 June 2001 <http://pc38.ve.weber.k12.ut.us/LegalNotice/VESCopyright.html>.

W3C Web Accessibility Initiative. 12 November 2000. 29 January 2001 <http://www.w3.org/WAI/>.

W3C Web Content Accessibility Guidelines 1.0. 29 January 2001 <http://www.w3.org/TR/WAI-WEBCONTENT/>.

Wallace, Jonathan and Mark Managn. *Sex, Laws and Cyberspace.* Henry Holt, 1997.

Warner, Mark, and Maureen Akins. "Training Today's Teachers for Tomorrow's Classrooms." *THE Journal.* October 1999. 2 October 2000. *Mastefile Premier, EBSCO.* #2562098.

Webopaedia. INT Media, 2001. 13 June 2001 <http://www.pcwebopaedia.com/>.

Wheaton, Joe E., et al. "Web Page Accessibility: A Forgotten Requirement for Distance Education." *Rehabilitation Education*, Summer 2001 (in press). 16 February 2001 <http://www.osu.edu/grants/dpg/articles.html>.

White, E. B. *Charlotte's Web.* Harper & Row, 1952.

Williams, Brad. *Web Publishing for Teachers.* IDG Books Worldwide, Inc., 1997.

Willams, Robin, and John Tollett. *The Non-Designer's Web Book. Second Edition.* Peachpit Press, 2000.

Winona School District 861. "Creating and Placing Web Pages." *Winona School District Guidelines.* February 1998. 13 February 2001 <http://wms.luminet.net/wmstechnology/861.WebPagesPolicy.html>.

Index

absolute link 83, 161, 165

absolute path 82, 83, 96

accessibility 33-35, 71, 90-93, 104-106, 116, 120, 136, 140-141, 146-147, 150-151, 161, 172-174

adaptation 50-51, 53, 91, 102

add-ons 158

Adobe Acrobat Reader 88, 91

advertising banner 34, 38, 78, 80, 99, 161, 165

affiliate programs 22-24, 29, 134

agreements, union 37

ALT attribute 90-91, 100, 140, 142, 161

ALT tag 90-91, 161

AltaVista 109

Alvirne High School 19

Amazon.com 22

American Biographies 5

Americans with Disabilities Act 34, 90

animations 53, 96

Applets 90

application service provider 63, 158

Arbor Heights Elementary School 37, 168

archive 19-20, 28, 37-38, 80, 122, 132, 152-154, 160-161

ASP, see application service provider

assignments 3, 18, 28, 37, 64, 123, 132

auctions 22, 24-25, 29, 134

audience
    primary 9, 92, 116
    secondary 9-11, 107, 116

audio clip 41, 79, 81, 161

authoring page tool 76, 78, 80, 82-83, 91, 161

authority 61, 72, 78, 103-104, 135, 144, 151

background images 97, 142

bandwidth 36, 81, 139, 161

banner, see advertising banner

Barnes and Noble 22

Berne Convention 49, 50

Beuselinck, Cynthia iv, v, vii

bit 161, 164-165

blinking text 99, 100, 142

Bobby 34, 93, 147

bookmark 96

browser 33-34, 36, 78-80, 83, 90-92, 96-101, 103, 106, 140, 147, 157-158, 161, 161, 163-165, 167

Buckman School 22

Calgary Board of Education iv, v, 36, 40, 67, 168

Carroll, Lewis 49, 168

cascading style sheets 86, 91, 97, 140, 161

CBT, see computer-based training

cell 98, 161

censorship 68-70

Center for Advanced Technologies in Education (CATE) 37, 45, 169

CGI script, see common gateway interface script

CGIs 35

charity programs 23, 29, 134

Charlie and the Chocolate Factory 7, 169

Charlotte's Web 13, 174

Clarke, Arthur C. 75, 167

collaborations 5-6, 20, 22, 28, 29

color 91, 98, 100-102, 142, 143, 152, 156, 163-164, 167-168, 170

common gateway interface script 161

communications 3, 36, 55, 69, 71, 156-159, 169

community connections 1, 2

compression tools 78, 124, 161

computer-based training 66

computer ethics 42, 161

connectivity 75, 82, 139, 161

consistency 32-34, 70

contact information 16, 32-33, 52, 56, 65, 67, 86, 97, 119, 129, 135, 144, 151, 162

content 13, 97
    collecting 86
    commercial 2, 38-39, 53, 122, 135, 151
    creating 86, 103-105
    fund-raising 2, 22
    guidelines 35, 38
    inappropriate 68
    quality 143
    requirements 121
    responsibility for 69
    restrictions 37, 46, 76, 121-122, 172
    team 119

copyright v, 11-12, 14, 18, 20, 22, 28-29, 32-33, 37, 40, 42-47, 49-59, 70-71, 85-86, 91, 95, 97, 100-101, 105-106, 118, 120, 121, 123, 124, 131, 137-138, 142, 144, 151, 162, 168-171, 173
    Canadian copyright links 58-59
    penalties for breaking 55

Crofton House School 95

CSS, see cascading style sheets

curricular web pages and sites 14, 18-20, 23-24, 132

Dahl, Roald 7, 169

date formats 33, 120

deep linking 54, 104, 137

design guidelines 33-36, 87-106, 120, 140

DHTML 35, 161

directory 10, 16. 26. 39, 46, 89, 129, 149, 157, 161, 165-166
Disabilities Rights Laws, A Guide to 34
disclaimer 35, 47, 161
display, see public display
digital audio transmissions 50-51
digitized image 43, 161
directories, staff and student 37
disclaimers 47
distribution 50-51
DNS, see domain name system 162
DNS server 83, 162
domain 44, 49, 50-51, 53, 57, 162
domain name system 162
download 3, 31, 50. 78, 81,88. 90-91, 96, 99, 100, 103, 105, 142, 151, 154, 156-159, 162, 165
download time 31, 33-34, 81, 90, 96, 99, 103, 105, 136, 142, 151, 157, 162
   minimizing 34, 105
Dryden, John 107, 169
education online 89, 160
Einstein, Albert 87
e-libraries 18-19, 35-36
evaluation x, 15, 28, 35, 88-89, 103, 106-107, 110-111, 135, 140, 147, 150-151
Evans Elementary School 19
executable 82, 162
extension 81, 98, 139, 145-146, 162
FTP, see file transfer protocol
fact page 19, 28, 86, 132
fair use 49-51, 54
file extension 98, 162
file size 34, 36, 78-79, 80, 81, 99, 140, 142, 162
   maximum 34
file type 33, 78, 151, 162
   restricting 35, 121
file transfer protocol 82, 162
flash 96, 162
focus group 10, 85
folder ix, 53, 76, 80,-82, 89, 137, 146, 161-162, 164
font 33-34, 101-102, 105, 143, 157, 162
font family 102, 143, 162
font styles 33-34
footer 47, 104-105, 120, 162
form handler 162
formats 33, 81, 99, 103, 105, 120, 122, 142, 144, 161, 164
404 error page 83, 162
frames 54, 91, 96, 105, 137, 163, 170
Friends of the Library 2, 35
functional formats 99
fund raising, see revenue generation
fund-raising links 24

gateways 18, 19, 35, 132
GIF 99, 163
glossary viii, x, 50, 161
goals ix, 8-9, 12, 16, 26, 35, 71, 85-86, 124-129
Google 21, 57, 109
Gotha Middle School 5
graphics 14, 33-34, 36, 42-43, 52, 54, 64, 69, 72, 78, 80, 87, 89-90, 99-100, 104, 106, 119-120, 124, 135, 139-140, 144, 147, 151. 156.-157, 161, 163, 167
graphics interchange format 163
graphics tools 78, 124
Guide to Disabilities Rights laws, A 34
guidelines, see publishing guidelines
hackers 68
handouts 18, 27-28, 108, 132
hardware reviews 155
header 120, 163
hexadecimal code 163
hexadecimal color chart 101, 163
hierarchical structure 92, 94, 163
Hillsboro School District 32, 38, 41, 44, 46, 170
hit counter 139, 163
home page 14-15, 33, 36, 47, 54, 64, 81, 87, 92, 95, 98, 100, 139, 141, 144, 163, 165
host 21, 62, 64, 70, 72, 85, 89, 163
host name 82, 163
hosting services 38, 64, 77
hot links 19, 28, 132
HTML, see hypertext markup language
hyperlink 47, 163-164, 167
Hyperstudio 29, 81, 105
hypertext 163
hypertext markup language 50, 54, 61, 67, 78, 86, 124, 137, 142, 163
image map 33, 90-91, 95, 106, 140, 163
image use 53, 97, 142
informative web pages and sites 14-17, 23-24, 26-28, 129-131
interactive tutorial 19
interconnected structure 94, 163, 167
   hierarchical web structure 92
   linear web structure 94
interface with databases 6
interlacing 99
Internet iv, vii-ix, 1,3, 9-10, 12, 18-21, 23-24, 27-28, 31, 32, 36-37, 39-40, 43, 45, 47-53, 55-58, 62-65, 67-69, 75-77, 79, 80, 82-83, 86, 88-90, 93-96, 100, 102-103, 106-107, 109, 155-156, 158, 162-169,171-173
Internet Explorer 7, 91-92, 147, 161, 164
Internet service provider 55, 63, 82, 163-164
Intranet 18, 36-37, 39, 47, 63, 68, 81, 121, 163-164, 168-169

inverted pyramid style 108, 144

ISP, see Internet service provider 63-65, 70, 139, 163-164

Jabberwocky 49, 57

Java 35, 63, 164

Javascript 35, 55, 57, 91, 140, 156, 164

Jordan, Michael 61, 170

JPEG (joint photographic expert group) 36, 99, 164

JPG, see JPEG

lashing test 99

Lawrence (KS) High School 103

layout 32-33, 76, 90-91, 96-97, 99, 103, 119, 141

legibility 101-102

liability ix, 12, 32, 39-40, 43, 55-56, 70, 122, 171-172

    online service providers 55-56, 138

linear structure 94, 164

link 2, 4-5, 13-14, 20, 22, 26, 30, 33, 35-36, 47, 52-54, 56-57, 76, 78-79, 83, 89, 92, 95-96, 99, 101, 103-104, 110, 137, 141, 143-144, 147, 149, 157, 161, 163-168

link checker 157, 164

link libraries 35

link rot 83, 164

linking 1, 4, 38, 40, 54, 76, 80, 83, 86, 96, 103-104, 135-136, 137

Linux 154, 164

listserv 17, 27, 131, 155, 164

loading

    responsibilities 118

    restrictions ix, 82, 139

log analysis 79, 157-158

Logan, Deb iv, v, vii, 66, 89

logos 34, 38, 54, 80, 96, 101-102, 120, 137, 141

long-term goals 85

Macintosh OS 164

maintenance x, 32, 38, 76-79, 83-84, 88. 103, 107, 110-111, 122, 124, 126, 152, 164

maintenance tools 78, 164

management tools 78

medium-range goals 85

meetings online 6

menu 14, 95-96, 98, 142, 144, 164

meta tag 57, 109, 138, 149, 164

Mill Hill School 97

Milne, A. A. vii, 172

Minnetonka (MN) Public Schools 2

mono, see monographic sound

monographic sound 105

Montgomery County Public Schools 6, 39, 66, 172

motion media 53

Mt. Laurel Hartford School 3

Mt. Pleasant (NC) Elementary School 21

moving web pages 83

multimedia 3, 4, 19-20, 22-23, 29, 34, 53, 79-81, 103, 105, 133, 139, 144, 162, 164-165, 168, 170, 173

museum 19, 28, 58, 132, 155

music 14, 27, 50, 53, 161, 169

naming convention 33, 76, 81, 97, 164

naming files and folders 80-81, 97, 164

navigation 32-33, 79,-80, 91-92, 95-97, 99, 136, 141-142, 151, 164

navigation tools 14, 33, 90, 97-98, 144, 164

Netscape 77, 79, 91, 92, 139, 147, 157, 161, 164

network 10, 22, 24, 32, 45, 53-54, 66, 67-68, 70, 72, 75-76, 82, 89, 155, 161, 163, 164

newbie 95, 164

newsgroup 165

Northmount School 18

objectives ix, 11-12, 16, 18, 28, 85-86, 128-129, 132

online auctions 22-23, 29, 134

online charity programs 23, 29, 134

online directory 39, 165

online map creation tool 165

online meetings 6

online service providers liability 55-56, 138

online shopping 23-25

Opera 79, 165

organizations and help for Web builders 155

orphan page 165

Othello 1, 173

page layout 96-97, 141, 165-166

parents vii, 1-3, 5-10, 15-18, 21-24, 32-33, 39-41, 43, 45, 68, 70, 89, 97, 107-109, 131, 149, 168, 171

    educational options 3

    partnerships with 1, 3, 170

password 3, 16-17, 19, 22, 26, 51-52, 69, 81, 118

path name 82-82, 90, 165

pathfinders 18-19, 28, 132

Pauli, Wolfgang 31

Payson (AZ) High School 4

PDF, see portable document format

performance, see public performance

permission forms ix, 17, 27, 42-44, 67, 123, 131

permission, written 20, 41-43, 51-52, 54, 105, 125, 137

personal information 21, 40-42, 68, 122-123, 151

photographs 37, 40-41, 43, 53, 122, 162

pixel 97-98, 165

plagiarism 37, 55, 57

platform 33, 77, 79, 154, 164-166

plug-ins 91, 105, 140, 144, 165

PNG (portable network graphic) 99, 165

policies, see publishing guidelines

Pope, Alexander 85, 172

portable document network 91, 101

portable network graphic, see PNG 165

portal 18, 19, 28, 35, 75, 77, 165

Portland (OR) Public Schools 22

PowerPoint 81, 94, 105

practice tests 19, 132

press release 108

primary audience 9, 116, 117

privacy 4, 32, 38, 40-41, 68

project page 19, 28, 132

promotion x, 9, 47, 107-109, 125, 148-149

proprietary 78, 165

public display 50-51

public performance 50-51

publicity 107-108, 125, 148

publishing
    staff work 43-45
    student work 40, 42-45, 53, 123
    volunteers' work 43-45

publishing guidelines ix, 2, 12, 15, 20-22, 31-48, 53, 67-68, 70, 72, 75, 84, 90, 119-123, 165, 169-170
    responsibility for 69

publishing policies, see publishing guidelines

push page 96, 165

putback 56

puzzles 19, 28, 132

RGB 101, 163, 165, 167

readability 34, 99, 101-103, 104, 135, 151, 161

reading lists 18, 28, 132

reference pages 83, 152, 165

relative link 166

relative path 82-83, 96

removing web pages or sites 76, 83, 152

reproduction 50-51

research investigations, see Webquests

resource sites 126, 149, 154

responsibility guidelines 45-47

restrictions ix, 33-34, 37, 39, 46, 48, 52-55, 67, 75- 76, 80, 82-83, 121-122, 137, 139, 146, 151, 172

retention period 35, 38, 80, 122, 166

revenue generation ix, 2, 14, 22-25, 134

reverse directory 166

reviews, software and hardware 155

revision viii, 33, 39, 45, 107, 110-111

rubrics 18, 28, 132

rules, see publishing policies

Rusk (TX) Independent School District 18

safety iii, vii, ix, 12, 20, 32, 37, 39-40, 43, 70, 122

St. Michael's School 15

scavenger hunts 19, 28, 132

school site awards 159

script 35-36, 38, 68, 72, 76, 82, 139, 161-162, 164

search engine 19, 21, 28, 54, 57, 79, 90, 109-110, 126, 149, 166

search tool 20, 33, 56-57, 79, 109-110, 149, 165, 166

secondary audience 9-11, 92, 107, 116

security, responsibility for 68, 118

serverix, 35, 38, 41, 44, 46, 53, 62-65, 67-68, 70, 72,-73, 77-83, 105-106, 114, 118, 125, 139, 157-159, 162, 166

server administrator 62-63, 79, 82-83, 166

Shakespeare, William 1, 173

shop-to-give programs 23, 134

short-term goals 86

showcase web pages and sites 14, 20-24, 29, 133

showcasing student work 4, 5, 14, 20-24, 29, 52

simulation 4, 19, 132

site structure 90, 92, 141, 166

software archives 154

software reviews 155

software tools ix, 77

sound recordings, see digital audio transmissions

space allocation ix, 79, 139, 166

special characters 80-81, 166

spelling lists 18, 28, 32

splash page 96, 166

stakeholders 2, 8, 66, 106

statistics ix, 77-79, 103, 110, 129, 148, 157, 166

statistics reporting tools 78, 166

storyboarding 95, 119

streaming audio 91, 105

streaming video 105, 140

summaries attributes 91, 140

support specialists 65, 67

survey 10,17, 27, 50, 85, 88, 110, 131, 150

syntax 78

syntax checker 78, 166

table 54, 91, 97-99, 100-101, 140, 161, 166

takedown 56

team, web planning ix, 7-8, 11-12, 62, 71-73, 77, 85, 110, 114-115, 124-126

technical guidelines 33-36, 72, 75-84, 139

template 33, 97, 98, 105, 141, 166

tests, practice 19

text 33-34, 36, 42, 44, 54, 56-57, 78, 90-91, 95, 98-103, 106, 138, 140, 142-143, 161-164, 166

Through the Looking Glass 49, 168

thumbnail 34, 90-91, 99, 142, 166

training, responsibility for 66, 118, 124

tutorial 19, 28, 66, 77, 79, 94-95, 110, 132

Uniform Resource Locator, see URL

union agreements 37

Universal Resource Locator, see URL

Unix 79, 156, 164-166
upload 45, 62, 67, 70, 76, 82, 166
uploading, responsibility for 70, 76
URL 14, 52, 80-83, 104, 110, 135, 144, 161, 166
validation tools 157
Victoria School of Performing and Visual Arts 4
video clip 79, 81
virtual tour 19, 28-29, 132
vision statement ix, 8, 11, 13-14, 26, 85-87,
    116-117
vocabulary lists 18
vortal, see portal 166
WBT, see web-based training
web-based training 68
web browser, see browser
web evaluation 88-89, 103, 140
web page
    authoring tools, 61, 67, 76, 78, 81-82, 91, 99
    basics 14
    content guidelines 35-38, 69
    creating 6-10, 15, 42, 48, 67, 102
    curricular 14, 18-20
    design guidelines 33-36, 87-106
    essential elements ix, 14
    generation services 64
    informative 14-17
    planning 7, 62, 101, 114-115, 124-126, 150
    project page 19, 28, 132
    resource cites 126, 149, 154
    responsibility guidelines 45-47
    revenue generation ix, 14, 22-25, 134

    showcase 14
    types 14
Webquests 4, 18, 20, 28, 88, 96, 132, 156
web safe colors 101, 167
web server, see server
web site
    community resource 2
    maintenance tools 78
    management tools 78
    marketing tool, use as 2, 4
    ownership 33, 42, 44, 53, 56-57
    protecting 21, 48, 56, 58, 138
    resources 10
    revenue source 2, 14, 22-25
    showcasing student work 4, 5, 14, 20-22, 52
    statistics 79
    statistical tools 78
    structure 92
web structure, see interconnected structure
web teams ix, 7, 20, 33, 45, 61, 71-73, 82, 110,
    114-115, 124-126
White, E. B. 13, 174
white space 33, 167
Windows 79, 154, 156, 162-163, 165, 167
Wonka, Willy 7
works cited list 168
World Wide Web (WWW) 4, 10, 36, 38-39, 41, 43-
    44, 46, 89, 98, 157, 161, 163, 167, 169, 171-172
WWW, see World Wide Web 34-35, 162-164, 167-168
WYSIWYG 167
Yahoo 10, 25, 57, 109, 155-156, 158

Notes

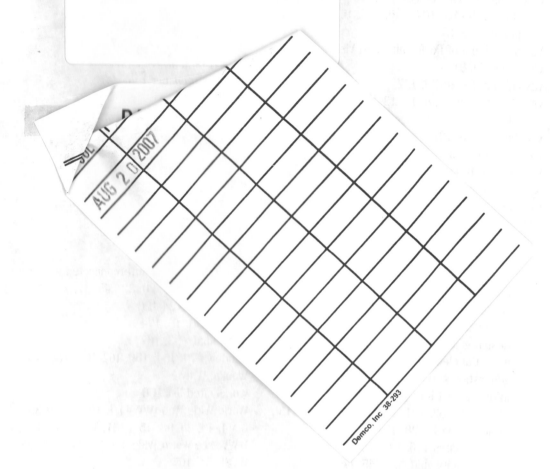